# LIVING WITH GHOSTS

To those forgotten in the rage of our 'wars',
in the hope that, one day,
they will be properly remembered.

**Brian Rowan** is a former BBC correspondent in Belfast. Since the late 1980s, he has reported on all the major developments on Northern Ireland's journey from war to peace; stories he has told using a range of sources – IRA, loyalist, police, military, intelligence, political, Church and others. Rowan left the BBC in 2005, the year the IRA ended its armed campaign. Four times he has been a category winner in the Northern Ireland Press and Broadcast awards, including twice as Specialist Journalist of the Year. He still comments and writes regularly on the issue of legacy and on the questions relating to the conflict period, and his analysis is often sought on the troubled politics of peace. Reviewing his last book, *Political Purgatory*, the commentator Alex Kane wrote: 'Rowan takes us up to and through the last crisis step by step. He doesn't do broad brush, big picture stuff. He hears the rustles, he observes the seeming trifles, he talks to the horses' mouths rather than third- or fourth-hand sources.' *Living With Ghosts* is Rowan's seventh book on the conflict and peace periods.

# LIVING WITH GHOSTS

## THE INSIDE STORY FROM
## A 'TROUBLES' MIND

## BRIAN ROWAN

MERRION
PRESS

First published in 2022 by
Merrion Press
10 George's Street
Newbridge
Co. Kildare
Ireland
www.merrionpress.ie

978 1 78537 403 6 (Paper)
978 1 78537 416 6 (Ebook)

A CIP catalogue record for this book is
available from the British Library.

Typeset in Minion Pro 12/17 pt

Front cover: Picture of Brian Rowan © Elle Rowan

Cover design by kvaughan.com

Merrion Press is a member of Publishing Ireland.

# CONTENTS

# Inside a 'Troubles' Mind

THIS IS A BOOK THAT has been in the different drawers and compartments of my head for quite some time. I struggled with when to write it or if to write it. It's a story that stretches out beyond the often strict boundaries of news into the dilemmas and arguments behind its scenes – the questions and, at times, the fears. It goes behind the headlines of some of the biggest stories to explain some of the challenges that are not often seen or heard. It explores how, when you live in the conflict, know its people and live with the dead, the responsibility of reporting becomes a much heavier weight to carry. Our story is the war of lies and that Holy Grail of 'truth'. An expedition along a never-ending road; walking through the war in search of something that might not be there.

In this place, we try to forget as much as we remember. But the mind's wardrobe is not so kind. I have said many times that it doesn't allow us to throw things out. It stores and holds on to detail. The conversations, the codewords, the statements and, in one specific case, the bodies I cannot forget seeing. Standing not far from the dead and not wanting to be there. This was our hell – where we were before this thing that we now call peace. That wardrobe I describe is not a hanging place for well-worn shirts or a dusty corner for broken shoes. It is a memory bank wired into the 1980s, 1990s and beyond, with a search mechanism that remembers everything and that repeats too much. Nothing is discarded. There is no charity shop which will take this stuff away. Stuff like the statement produced from down the trousers of an IRA contact, the man called 'P. O'Neill', in a street meeting in 1988 not long after gun and bomb attacks in the Netherlands had added to the body-count of his 'war'; and years later, a stone's throw from my then workplace at the BBC in Belfast, a conversation over coffee with a loyalist leader explaining the latest codeword as if we were talking about doughnuts or scones or milk or butter. How 'normal' it all became, when everything was far from normal, and how I allowed myself to become a part of that.

The man I was meeting for that coffee, a former soldier, was by then part of the leadership of the Ulster Defence Association (UDA). In the throes of a loyalist killing surge and rage in the early 1990s, he told me there had been a search of the dictionary, looking, I was told, for something that would encapsulate or capture that phase of the conflict to use as a codeword. They settled on 'the crucible' – meaning the crucible of war, summing up how the temperature was rising. These codewords were a means of authenticating contacts between the UDA-linked Ulster Freedom Fighters

(UFF) and the media; either the first or the last words in often 'anonymous' phone calls to news organisations to make a threat or to put their name or stamp to some bomb or bullet or killing or warning. I would hear and read those two words – the crucible – many times; I can still hear that coin-box voice at the other end of the line. In that phase of the conflict, that codeword was used to condemn the talks between political leaders John Hume and Gerry Adams, to threaten what loyalists called the pan-nationalist front and, on one occasion, to warn of an intensification of violence 'to a ferocity never imagined'. This statement was on the eve of 1993, a year when Northern Ireland was dragged to its very edge. We were witnessing a killing frenzy, a madness. Living in times of no hope, or so it seemed.

There is a blindness in war. Our vision deteriorates. It becomes impaired.

When I started to scribble the first words of this book, a friend, an academic, Dr Jonny Byrne, asked me if there would be a chapter on ethics. It sounded like an invitation to step inside some moral maze, to engage in some self-examination of right and wrong, to open the wardrobe and to let the detail spill out – there for all to see and to judge. As best I could, I had talked with all sides. I believed it was the right thing to do. This meant talking with the 'terrorists'. You don't report a conflict by ignoring some of those who are part of the fight. For me, this book is an explanation, not a confession. It is a walk along that thinnest of lines that I have often described, those between life and death, and on a path where morals, ethics and principles become blurred and our minds become tortured – what the Queen's University academic Dr Joanne Murphy called 'a journalistic grey zone'. We can close the door, but it is still there. It is also the making of a jigsaw puzzle, as the statements of war fade and those in the fight reach for new words that become the beginnings of some 'peace'; the start of some looking in another dictionary, and how they would come to express themselves differently. How, over time, guns became quieter and hope became louder – whispered at first, until it found its voice.

This can't be my 'tell-all' story. I'll leave that somewhere to be read years from now. But it can be a 'tell-more' story. At times, I'm writing about fear – personal fear – living and thinking inside that 'Troubles' mind. The nightmares. Shouting in my sleep, trapped, surrounded. The dilemmas. The decisions. The doubts. Trying to stay strong, but losing my nerve for a while, needing to escape. And how I still fall into places and moods of darkness.

I know only too well the brokenness of people here, how they suffered, what they lost. I have heard many of their stories. I survived and have not gone anywhere to have a label or a description attached to my fears or to that darkness I can get lost in. Nor have I asked for the healing potions that might help. There is something about reporting conflict, this war on our doorsteps, this thing that was so close to us, that said to me, and still says to me, that you have to lock this stuff in some safe inside yourself. Use the combination numbers to protect sources. Protect information. Protect those around you. Manage all of that.

My colleague and friend Mervyn Jess likens it to being alone inside 'an airtight container'. He is right. There was a loneliness in the secretiveness of it all. I haven't spoken or written much about it. But, in an interview for the *Scéalta* series in 2021, I described a sense of being both physically and mentally broken as I left the BBC in 2005. That is how I felt. Wrecked. I no longer wanted to be on radio and television. At times I struggled to speak my words, to record my voice.

It took Jess until 2022 to tell me that some of those closest to me thought I was having 'some sort of a meltdown'. They were kind enough not to say anything at the time. I don't know if I would use the term 'meltdown', but I was experiencing something. I had breathed in too much of this stuff. I was weighed down, certainly – perhaps broken down. The previous twenty years or so had taken their toll; a cumulative wearing down in terms of constant pressures.

The person who knows most about this is my wife. There are secrets in reporting conflict, things you can't talk about. You become afraid of talking in your sleep, so I spoke with Val. This was something that Joe Austin touched on in that *Scéalta* interview, when he thought back into that conflict period and asked: 'How does she keep you sane, when the world around you is insane?' He was reading my mind and found a question I often ask myself. At times, just having Val there to listen was all I needed – an important second opinion.

# PROLOGUE

# 'They'll never find it'

I NEEDED A FRIEND TO get rid of something – my detailed source notes relating to the break-in at a police Special Branch office at Castlereagh in Belfast and the political intelligence-gathering scandal that came to be known as 'Stormontgate'. In 2002 the IRA was linked to both events and denied involvement in both. I didn't believe them then. I don't believe them now. Some years after these events, the British Security Service, MI5, was seeking pre-publication access to a book I was writing at that time. There had been correspondence, and I had taken advice. It was 2008, three years after I had felt the need to escape from the story of our past, and I was back in a tug-of-war. There could be a raid or a search of my home. I was told to get the information out of the jurisdiction.

In my continuing research on those 2002 events, I had obviously trespassed into the intelligence world, discovered too much about a bugging and surveillance operation that was part of the response to Stormontgate, and found out about a Special Branch 'source', who opened the door to the IRA's secrets. MI5 was also concerned about what I might write about agents operating at the top of loyalist organisations. The letters sent to me were from solicitors acting, I was informed, on behalf of Her Majesty's Government. One, which came by registered post and was dated 31 January 2008, stated: 'My client is concerned that your book might contain information that would put lives in danger and/or be damaging to national security. Without access to the manuscript my client cannot be more specific but my letter to you dated 10 January 2008 highlights an example of the sort of information that if published might have this effect.' In the letter of 31 January, I was encouraged 'to obtain independent legal advice as soon as possible'.

Requests for access to the manuscript became a demand, and the need to get my notes out of the way was now pressing. I contacted two journalist friends to ask if they would take them. The first, Mervyn Jess, thought that he was far too obvious. His would be the first place they would come looking. I then called Seamus Kelters, another colleague from my days at the BBC. Within hours, he was at my home. We took a walk, without phones, and I explained my predicament. When we got back to the house, he asked me to tape shut the box into which I had placed my files. He put it in his car, left and, in a brief telephone conversation that evening, assured me: 'They'll never find it.' I pictured him burying it in deep ground, muck up to his oxters. But, years later, after his death from cancer, I was told he had hidden the box in plain sight. We survive on humour. I joke with Jess that in this moment of need I discovered the difference between a Catholic friend and a Protestant friend. It's something that, in all the seriousness of that moment, we can laugh about and that Kelters would laugh about if he was still here.

The real learning I took from the official letters was that the 'war' might be over, but efforts to bury its secrets continued, and continue even today. MI5 wanted the manuscript for the purpose of redaction. These are the new battles being fought on all sides; the long fight in the peace to hide uncomfortable truths.

This incident also confirmed to me that you can't just walk away – it is not that easy. This was something I realised very quickly after leaving the BBC. We are living with ghosts, a phrase used by Dr Joanne Murphy in an interview with me in 2021, when she described how we are 'constantly pulled back to what are environments of huge pain'. For my own part, in the conflict period, I was speaking with sources on all sides who knew the details of numerous killings. That's how close I got. And these many years later, I know more about the sick acts that have left us in that place of shadows and ghosts – still, at times, afraid of talking in our sleep.

I struggle to explain how I became involved in coverage of that war. It was not a road that I had planned to travel. I left school at an early age. I could run a bit then, and I ran a couple of times for Northern Ireland. I was interested in the detail of athletics and, for a while, I was a member of the UK-wide National Union of Track Statisticians and became involved with the then Northern Ireland Amateur Athletics Association. I remember how in 1981 Olympic champion Steve Ovett saved the UK Athletics Championships on the Antrim Forum track, competing when others stayed away. They were frightened by the news of the hunger strike at the Maze prison and the headlines of the street violence that resulted from that. The veteran Belfast journalist Jim McDowell was, at the time, an athletics correspondent at the *News Letter* and I have the piece he wrote, composed in his very distinctive style:

> The biggest hush-hush athletics operation in the history of the game here turned what were, candidly, the nine-carat UK Closed Championships at Antrim into twenty-four-carat Olympic gold. The jewel of a meeting jaundiced by withdrawals because of Ulster's political trauma jetted in late yesterday afternoon. His arrival had been kept a close secret by the athletics hierarchy, but when Moscow Olympics gold medallist Steve Ovett trotted out onto the track at Antrim Forum for the last event of yesterday's GRE Games, the atmosphere among a 5,000 festival crowd [*sic*] basking in bright sunshine was as intoxicating as poteen.

What McDowell was writing about was what I was interested in. The big milers of that era: Ovett, John Walker, Eamonn Coghlan, Seb Coe. I was scribbling a few words for a number of athletics magazines and, later, McDowell opened doors for me. Initially I was to provide some coverage of track and field and cross-country for two Belfast newspapers and was then given a training opportunity as a sub-editor. That came out of the blue. Years later, McDowell told me he recognised something in me – that interest in facts and figures and analysis. He could see some wider potential. It was something I hadn't thought about. Then I worked in a press agency, learning alongside him. Without him, my career in journalism would not have happened.

Long before any meetings with the IRA and the loyalist organisations, I had reported from two World Cross-Country Championships: Gateshead in 1983 and Lisbon in 1985. Carlos Lopes and Zola Budd were the winners at the latter championships in what was an electric atmosphere. What, then, made me want to talk to the IRA, the loyalists and those in security, military and intelligence, all of them dug into the different corners and trenches of that conflict period?

Part of it, I think, was a journey of discovery linked to what we as a family had experienced in the early 1970s. Like so many others, we were forced from our home. There had been a period of attacks and intimidation. We still talk about a particular incident in that period: being at Mass when the windows of the church came falling in – shattered by bricks or bottles. In the dark, cars had also been damaged. I remember the priest opening a door to look outside. My sister, Roisin, who was eight at the time, still talks about how she thought she was going to die.

Our family experience is a tiny jigsaw piece in a much bigger picture. I remember men in combat jackets speaking with my mother at the door of our home, telling her we would be all right, that we had nothing to fear from them. But the attacks on our home continued until we had to leave – leave a house that had wire grilles on its front windows. At times, it felt like we were living in a cage. Perhaps this explains, in part at least, some of my interest in finding out more – how it started, why I took those difficult steps into that conflict arena and into a world of secrets. Then, I suppose, the news took over – a fascination with this war that was on our doorstep, that was so close to us all, that sucked us in.

As I look back, it is not about one side. It is about all the sides. Not just about who started it, but why it started. Unless we try to understand it all, we understand nothing. We stay lost and trapped in our own opinions. And, more than that, we shovel those opinions on top of others, damaging them. It is such a sin.

In 2003 the former Sinn Féin publicity director Danny Morrison was writing about a book I had just published, *The Armed Peace*. He talked about those steps I took in the 1980s, away from sport and into this other world. How I 'moved on and established a reputation for breaking news stories, particularly for exclusives on IRA GHQ claims of responsibility for major operations and, later, during the peace process, IRA leadership policy statements'.

What started for me in the late 1980s was a whole new experience. It is different now. I no longer have to go to the

IRA and the loyalist organisations and others for the statements and explanations of war, for their words on the dead and wounded. But the past is not over, not yet. For some, not ever. There is this continuing scrutiny of what happened and why. The mysteries. The questions. The silence. The dead. The injured. The sickness. The brokenness of it all. It broke me at times. But I better understand now. Most importantly, I understand why it should never be repeated.

P. O'Neill has gone quiet. The loyalist codewords have fallen into disuse. The landscape has been demilitarised. So, there is a space now to think some more and to explain some more. For me, this is the purpose of the pages that follow. Of course, with age and time, wrinkles appear in the memory and in the mind, so I have used my extensive archive notes and statements and interview transcripts to do my best to recall events, times and dates as accurately as possible. I've gone back to some people to try to get a better understanding of then and now. This is my story from a period in our wars and of a time when we found a way to peace. What I thought then and what I think now. Knowing, also, that sometimes we can think too much.

## ONE

# The IRA

### *My First Contact with P. O'Neill*

I LIT A FIRE IN the backyard of my home, to burn statements in which you could count the dead. Enniskillen 11, Gibraltar 3, Holland 3, Lisburn 6, Mill Hill 1, Ballygawley 8, the number often determining for how long we would remember or how quickly we would forget. It was late 1988. The conflict was approaching its twentieth year. By now, many had seen all they wanted to see and heard all they wanted to hear. I can imagine televisions being switched off, or the volume being turned down. Only tuning back in when something more shocking than the 'usual' would demand attention. But this up-close reporting was new to me. New, in terms of those statements and how I came to have them. They were from my first contacts with P. O'Neill in the late 1980s. I would come to know five people by that name and in that role of authorised spokesperson for the IRA leadership. None of them were related, but all used the same name. They spoke of war before they came to speak of peace.

8

My contact with two of them spans the period from the late 1980s through to the late 1990s. One was a well-known public figure, now in his late sixties; the other was very much a man of the shadows, certainly in that time. Today, he is in his mid-sixties. Occasionally, I still meet and speak with both of them, P. O'Neill 1 and P. O'Neill 2, often thinking back to some of those statements from the war that were part of a dark text of death. Their knowledge is considerable, fine-detailed, but not yet an open book. Those parts that still have implications in the here and now remain closed – something worth thinking about when we talk about 'truth' and how it might be achieved. Already, so much critical memory is gone from people no longer with us.

Despite that fire I lit, an old work log has helped me retrace some of the steps to those first statements, the ones I burned. It dates to 1987–8, when this place lived and died in an atmosphere of poison and tension. It was bent out of shape, broken. It could, I suppose, be described as an illness of kinds, in which the abnormal became normal. How casual we were talking about the dead, about bombs and bullets. It was 'terrible', 'awful'. These were the words of everyday conversation, the labels attached to the latest news. News that often held our attention for only a fleeting moment, before something else or someone else needed our time.

My reading takes me back to the IRA statement the day after the Enniskillen Remembrance Day bomb. Then, months later, to a statement on the Gibraltar killings, where the SAS shot dead three unarmed members of the IRA: Seán Savage, Mairéad Farrell and Dan McCann.

This book is not just the story of the actual time, but also the now time – how with learning and experience we begin to see and think differently. So, not just the early excitement of news and being able to achieve a deep access to information, but also the dawning realisation of how quickly, or how easily, we forgot the dead. At the time of those IRA statements relating to Enniskillen and Gibraltar, I was twenty-nine. Old enough, but not nearly old enough to make sense of those events. Yet I think of something the Belfast republican Jim Gibney talks about later in this book – being interned at eighteen and in prison when his father died. How young this war was, with teenage soldiers on all sides who had no time to grow up, to think up, or to wise up. People were born into and thrown into the hell of this place.

Many years later, in a television documentary made in 2013, I was asked for my thoughts on those shootings in Gibraltar. There had been twenty-five years of learning since 1988 – proper time and space in which to think. 'They could have been arrested,' I said, 'but they were shot dead to send a message to the IRA, that if that's the game you want to play, these are the rules. It was about delivering a message into the face of the IRA.'

Time gives you context, more confidence to speak outside the parameters of pure news. I have an understanding, now, that conflict is not just about these separate incidents, about one day and then the next, but about how they link together.

How they join up. Nothing stands on its own. So the wars of this place have to be seen in that wider frame. Our story is not on one page, it is on many. Not three killings as in Gibraltar, but almost 4,000 deaths in some days that are never forgotten and others that are rarely remembered. This was a 'shoot-to-kill' war. It was not named as such, but that is what it was. The SAS did not take prisoners, nor did the IRA. Many who were unarmed were killed by all sides.

Back in the 1980s, there were numerous other statements on the bombs and the bullets and the so-called 'botched operations' of war. There were statements of apology, but in circumstances when sorry or regret became words of little meaning, especially when you look now at how frequently and regularly those statements were made. The pattern. The threads. The inevitability. In all wars, there will always be civilian casualties and fatalities. The conflict here was no different – civilians killed, collateral damage. A statement expresses some regret and the war moves on to the next killing, but the families of the dead stand still.

As I stoked that fire in my backyard, my neighbours then, Jack and Olive, must have wondered what was going on. What was I up to? This was at a time when the police were showing more interest than usual in a particular IRA statement. How I came to have it, the process of receiving it – these were questions I could not answer or, more accurately, would not answer. It was one of many moments when I had to navigate that moral maze; find my way out of situations; work out the right thing to do, even though many would consider it the wrong thing to do. I was freelancing at this time, and my work log tells me that I provided the statement to the BBC, Ulster Television, RTÉ, Downtown Radio, the Press Association, the *Irish Independent*, *The Irish News* and *The Irish Times*. There are no details of my contact with the IRA, whether it was in person or by telephone.

If I have recalled the moment correctly, the statement related to a bomb attack in England. The IRA had targeted the sleeping quarters at a barracks. One soldier was killed, others injured. That attack was in the Finchley constituency of Margaret Thatcher. Four years after bombing the Conservative Party Conference in Brighton and trying to kill the Prime Minister, the IRA was back in Britain and back in the headlines. It had put its name to the bomb. The words given to me became part of the coverage and part of the story. All of this explains the police interest in this particular statement.

I was still finding my way, working out the reporting of these things – this was a long way from the safe places of tracks and fields and running and jumping and throwing. This was a new learning curve. How to gather information relating to conflict. How to make and protect sources. How to stay on the right side of the many lines. There were no easy answers for a reporting task that many will never regard as being right or ethical. Their argument was: how could you talk with 'terrorists' and communicate with those involved in such acts? But if only it were that simple. You cannot report a conflict without having access to all the sides and to their thinking. And you should not report a conflict of this kind without having that access. War is not one story, but many stories – a clash of narratives and of lines.

I thought about it then. And I better understand it now. That need to build contacts across the lines: the five P. O'Neills; being able to speak with those at the top of the loyalist organisations – UDA, Ulster Volunteer Force (UVF), Red Hand Commando – and to a number of the army generals; the conversations I had with a string of chief constables – Sir Hugh Annesley, Sir Ronnie Flanagan, Sir Hugh Orde, Sir Matt Baggott, Sir George Hamilton – and many other officers up and down the ranks; some meetings with MI5; and occasionally meeting with secretaries of state, security ministers, officials at the Northern Ireland Office (NIO) and Irish government officials. And then with the political leaders, all of them different. There was more contact with some because of their links with others: the controllers and directors of prisons; Church people, particularly those in the Protestant community, who began that exploration of peace long before the unionist political leaders; working relationships with other journalists. I still have many of their numbers in my book or stored in my head. I do not keep contact details in my phone. I'm old-fashioned in that sense. All of this was learning in progress – criss-crossing those lines, cross-referencing them, trying to join up the dots. The wider the frame of contacts, the more corners you get to look in, the better you understand.

In the conflict period we could also become numb, dehumanised by the routine of killing. When it lasts so long, you get used to war. You can become almost indifferent, detached. Not uncaring, but, at times, not caring enough. I suppose it is part of losing ourselves in conflict. Our heads and our hearts not wanting or not being allowed to hold on to everything. Yet it is always there, if not at the front of our minds, then somewhere inside some of those deeper compartments. In 2022 I watched on television much of the early part of the Russian invasion of Ukraine. I listened to Clive Myrie, Orla Guerin, Lindsey Hilsum, Mark Austin, Lyse Doucet, Matt Frei, Alex Crawford, Jeremy Bowen, Sarah Rainsford and President Zelensky. Watched that terrifying ambush in which the *Sky News* team, including veteran correspondent Stuart Ramsay, had the luckiest of escapes. How close they came to death. I watched Putin until my anger made me switch him off. The slaughter and the destruction are on a completely different scale, of course, but my point is the same. We tune in until we can watch and listen no more. It becomes too much.

I imagine that in the decades-long conflict of this place many people could take no more, hear no more. That is when the dead became simply news and numbers, and I was part of that reporting. I remember how impersonal it was. How it included the next statement and, from some, the 'usual' condemnation. How, like the war itself, we quickly moved on to whatever was next. How the dead of yesterday were left behind as the dead of the next news or the next day moved centre stage. That is what I think about now – the ghosts with which we live.

That fire in my backyard, in the dark of some night in the late 1980s, was probably a moment of panic – not knowing what to do and doing something. Destroying words. Watching the particles and the ash dance in the smoke. Trying to burn away any trail, any evidence. Protecting information, protecting sources. Ethics, morals, right and wrong, blurred lines, wrong lines – who decides? There are few straight lines in war, and they are bent and twisted even more in peace.

In this same period, I was a researcher on the BBC *Panorama* documentary 'The Long War', working and learning with the veteran journalist Peter Taylor. I think it was in this period that I had my first proper conversation and meeting with Martin McGuinness, in an upstairs room at the Sinn Féin offices on Cable Street in Derry. I remember him calling someone else into the room and having a sense that that person was almost standing to attention. I would revisit those offices in the early 1990s for interviews with McGuinness, which, although not properly or fully understood by me then, included words from him that began to suggest he was thinking outside the frame of conflict. McGuinness knew much more than I did. Those fighting the war, at its coalface, had to think about how it might end – the possible steps towards a resolution, how to take them and when to take them; what words to use to help others with their steps.

A line jumped out from that Taylor film, spoken by a former Commander-in-Chief of Land Forces, General Sir

James Glover: 'In no way can or will the Provisional IRA ever be defeated militarily. The army's role has been now for some time, and I'm sure will continue to be, to help create the conditions whereby a full democratic, peaceful, political solution can be achieved.'

Throughout the 1980s Libya had been arming the IRA, and the latest shipments had included Semtex explosive. Beyond the film, we would see a build-up in IRA attacks targeting British soldiers. This was as we moved towards August 1989 and the twentieth year of the military presence. Although there was little talk of peace, there was some talking, the beginnings of something. It was not fully understood or believed then, but, eventually, it would make itself heard above the noise of conflict. However, all of this would take time. Time in which many more would lose their lives. Part of the negotiation of peace is an escalation of violence, so that you are talking from a position of strength – killing to prove it. There would be no white flag, no surrender from any side.

The stalemate of then is so much more obvious now. It was a war that, for all its weaponry and firepower, was going through the motions but going nowhere. People were dying in ditches so they wouldn't lose, knowing they could not win. There was nothing in what we could see then that would have allowed us to think seriously of peace. This had been particularly clear in the immediate aftermath of the Gibraltar shootings, a period which was terrifying. It started when a loyalist, Michael Stone, carried out a gun and grenade attack during the funerals of the three IRA dead at Milltown Cemetery. Three mourners were killed and dozens injured. Then, just days later, came the killing of two army corporals at another republican funeral, that of Caoimhín Mac Brádaigh, a member of the IRA and one of those killed by Stone. That attack became the backdrop to what happened next, the escalation in violence, with each incident trying to outdo the last in terms of how shocking it was.

After the Milltown attack, the IRA had been in contact with me. My work log has details of a statement and a video, the latter showing masked and armed members of that organisation in some final tribute to Mac Brádaigh. The BBC chose not to use the pictures, probably worried about the times we were in, so I brought the video to ITN in Belfast instead, this on the eve of the Mac Brádaigh funeral. It was included in their report.

I was not in Milltown cemetery when Stone carried out his attack. Nor was I at the Mac Brádaigh funeral that Saturday in March 1988, but I was in west Belfast a short time afterwards. On the Falls Road I met with the then P. O'Neill. My work log has a few words: 'IRA statement on Brady [Mac Brádaigh] funeral killings.' I also recorded a number of the headlines from the newspaper coverage the next day, including 'Murder by Mob' and 'Bloodlust takes Control'. The IRA statement was included in the stories of how the two army corporals, Derek Wood and David Howes, inexplicably drove into the funeral cortege, and how, in the rage that followed, they were dragged from their car, shot dead and left on waste ground. In the moment it happened, many would have feared they were witnessing another Stone-type incident.

A Clonard priest, Fr Alec Reid, tried desperately to save these men from the IRA. Photographs of him kneeling beside the bodies are amongst the most harrowing and haunting images of the conflict years. The 2013 documentary I referenced earlier and, in which I was asked about the Gibraltar shootings, was the story of those fourteen days in March 1988 when Northern Ireland, or the North, stood at the very edge and fell into something more frightening and sickening. Killing was commonplace. People not easily shocked were terrified. No one was going to survive in such circumstances.

In the documentary, the veteran Belfast journalist David McKittrick searched for and somehow found the words to describe the madness of 1988: 'People's fuses blew,' he said. What an image he created in those three words. He continued:

Nothing had really quite prepared you for this ... You had these three major violent events. You had all these deaths. You had the old rules being discarded. You had all these mysteries left about what exactly happened. What happened at Gibraltar? What happened with Michael Stone? What was he at? And what happened with the corporals? So, it was just a period of great destabilisation, of great shock.

Stone's attack was a public performance (something I would speak about with him many years later). And days after those killings in the cemetery, camera operators and photographers would capture all the ugliness of what happened to the corporals. What was different was seeing it actually happen in that news coverage. There was no hiding from the pictures – a visual reality of those 'terrible' and 'awful' events we so often discussed in such casual terms. We do not forget those days of 1988.

The *14 Days* documentary was made for the BBC by DoubleBand Films. It searched deep into the convulsion of those times to find another story and some hope: quiet conversations between John Hume and Gerry Adams, with Fr Reid involved. To borrow words from the former Presbyterian Moderator Dr Ken Newell, Reid was the 'electrician'. 'He took two wires where there was no current going across them,' Newell said, 'and he wrapped himself around, like tape around them, held them together, until the current of communication began to flow.' It was known that Hume and Adams were talking, that their parties were meeting. But we could not see its worth or potential. Certainly not then. There were too many other things blocking our vision. The IRA was active in a number of theatres: in Northern Ireland, in Britain and on mainland Europe.

On 1 May 1988, I wrote a few words into my work log: 'IRA statement on Holland'. That day, I had met with P. O'Neill on a street in west Belfast, somewhere above the Andersonstown and Glen roads. It was a Sunday. Hours earlier, three RAF personnel had been killed and others injured in gun and bomb attacks in the Netherlands. The statement related to those incidents. On his walk to meet me, P. O'Neill had concealed that statement down his trousers. These many years later, I thought I would try to further explore the mechanics of these communications – how they worked in the 1980s; how words travelled from the people involved in those operations and other such incidents to P. O'Neill back in Ireland and then to me or other journalists. But, nearly thirty-five years later, I got nowhere when I asked those questions. 'That's top secret,' was the response. 'No matter what way it's answered, it allows an insight into internal communications, but, also, it has personal implications.' With those words, I knew I was at the end of this particular exploration of the war. It wouldn't matter if we were talking about events fifty years previously – the answer would be the same: that there is still a lock on that drawer and no key to open it. It's part of what remains out of bounds – significant missing pieces in the truth or information jigsaws.

Back in 1988, just days after that Sunday morning meeting, there was another IRA statement on another bomb. This time the device was discovered underneath an army officer's car at a base in Germany. Such are the fine margins between life and death. My work log then takes me to the summer of 1988. To a bomb in Lisburn where six soldiers were killed. It was one of those 'headline' attacks when everyone becomes interested again in the running battles of this place. I had two IRA communications about this. Firstly, a phone contact in which I was told the IRA had placed the bomb. Then, the next day, at a meeting in west Belfast, I collected a more detailed statement, which I no longer have. It may well have been one of those I burned. From memory, neither of these contacts was directly with P. O'Neill.

As I continued to flick through the pages of the log, I read of an IRA attack on a helicopter in Crossmaglen and on a school bus in Fermanagh; bombs in Belfast, in Germany and on the border at Killeen; then the roadside bomb triggered to catch a bus carrying soldiers on the Ballygawley to Omagh road, which killed eight of them. With each line in that log, I remember something else about those days: maybe a name or a particular interview, an army sniffer dog that was killed, or some other detail. I am back in time. Back in that war. If there was something, anything, that the political talks of that time might have changed, it was lost or buried in those headlines of 1988 – that year when people's fuses blew; a year when there were no hints or clues of changing minds or changing words in the many statements of P. O'Neill.

I wrote earlier about how lines of apology enter the scripts, but how valueless and meaningless they become when the so-called 'mistakes' continue; continue because they are not mistakes but, rather, an inevitability of conflict or war situations. When the acclaimed Irish artist Colin Davidson painted 'Silent Testimony', an exhibition of eighteen portraits to tell the story, not of our past, but of the pain in the present, one of those who sat for him was Paul Reilly. Paul's daughter, Joanne, was killed in April 1989, a victim of one of those IRA mistakes. The sitting, twenty-six years after the bomb, was in Joanne's bedroom, kept exactly as it was at the time of her death. This is what I meant when I wrote that for families time stands still, but the war moves on to its next act.

Joanne was killed when a no-warning bomb exploded beside her office at a builder's yard where she was working. The target was the nearby police station in Warrenpoint. Her killing brought to twenty-nine the number of so-called 'mistakes' since the Enniskillen Remembrance Day bomb of November 1987. Numbers on a list. Names forgotten, except by those closest to the dead or when we are reminded, such as in the 'Silent Testimony' exhibition, which has now been viewed by over 100,000 people. It is a visual reminder, not just of where we were, but where we are.

At the time, the IRA's statement on Warrenpoint was an attempted explanation – words about two timing devices on the bomb, a description of a warning smoke grenade and 'a highly sensitive micro-switch which would detonate the bomb if … disturbed by the British Army's robot'. Then, the explanation of how the mistake occurred: 'one of our volunteers may have unintentionally disturbed the micro-switch'. It meant the bomb exploded not sixty minutes after it was placed, but after just fifteen minutes. The statement read: 'We offer our sincerest apologies to those bereaved and those injured.' Just weeks before the Warrenpoint bomb, then RUC Chief Constable Sir John Hermon had published his annual report, which included these words: 'the Provisional IRA has shown time and time again that their "mistakes" in killing and maiming civilians are an inevitable, unavoidable part of their campaign. They know it, and their apologies and explanations are fraudulent.'

In an old republican magazine, published in November 1988, there is a calendar of IRA attacks stretching from October 1987 through to October 1988. It is in small print across thirteen pages. I have made my own notes and attached them to a number of those pages, a few words on each: catastrophic consequences; deep regret; badly planned operation; deepest condolences; nothing we can say by way of comfort; stay well clear of all British personnel in Europe and Britain; operation went tragically wrong. My notes summarise a number of IRA statements, what they said after some of their mistakes.

In January 1989, just weeks before Joanne Reilly was killed, both the IRA and Gerry Adams spoke on this issue of civilian deaths. The statements were clearly choreographed. The IRA went first, on the eve of the Sinn Féin Ard-Fheis, where Adams would use his speech to speak directly to the 'active service volunteers of Óglaigh na hÉireann'. The IRA said:

> There is a greater realisation than ever of the need for the IRA to avoid civilian casualties. The fatalities of the past year occurred against a background of active service units stepping up attacks on crown forces and on establishment figures which put the British administration under more pressure than at any other

time since perhaps 1979. Unfortunately, through a combination of tragic circumstances, many civilians died in operations which dented the confidence of some of our supporters. We have tried to rectify the reasons why mistakes were made. Our main concern is the immensity of the human tragedy involved, and we realise the use which the British have made of these bad operations, and how demoralising they have been ... Whilst the leadership is responsible to the broad Republican Movement for the consequences and repercussions of IRA actions, all volunteers are subject to the leadership for their conduct of the war. When and where necessary that leadership has been exercised, inquiries have been undertaken, their recommendations acted upon, and as a result we hope to avoid many of the mistakes of the past ...

Those IRA words were printed on the front page of the *An Phoblacht* newspaper on Thursday, 26 January 1989, making and clearing a stage for Adams to think out and speak out on this matter at the Sinn Féin Ard-Fheis. In Dublin, he would speak words that he wanted the IRA to hear. 'You have a massive responsibility,' Adams said:

At times the fate of this struggle is in your hands. You have to be careful and careful again. These are the feelings of the broad mass of the republican people, feelings which are shared by republican activists and which now call for more circumspection than ever before. The morale of your comrades in jail, your own morale and of your comrades in the field can be raised or dashed by your actions. You can advance or retard this struggle. I say these words, not in the hypocritical condemnatory fashion of selective moralists in the churches or in the political establishment. I say them in solidarity and in comradeship. I am mindful that the media will misrepresent my remarks. I am aware that the hardy annuals of unfounded speculation about hawks and doves, splits and disagreements will be given yet another airing. For this reason, some of you may feel that some of those things should be left unsaid. I understand such sentiment, but it is a responsibility of leadership to lead from the front on this crucial issue as much as any other. Nothing I say should be interpreted as a condemnation of the IRA. The men and women volunteers of Óglaigh na hÉireann have my continued loyalty. As I remind them of their responsibilities, I salute them as freedom fighters.

Adams knew, and the IRA knew, that these interventions would be interpreted and misinterpreted by others, that they would bring media and political attention to a series of actions that republicans would much rather forget – not just attention, but a scrutiny and a condemnation, as well as that commentary about 'hawks and doves' and those tugs-of-war inside the republican movement. Yet it was said. 'There was a necessity to say it,' a source familiar with those developments commented. This was in conversation in 2022, thinking back to the 1980s and the importance or imperative of 'getting that message through'. But, when it happens again, then the message, for all its weight, is reduced to just more words. To the same-old.

Just a matter of weeks later, the bomb in Warrenpoint was proof that these mistakes could not be rectified, that the 'bad operations' were part of the norm, that the 'armed struggle' could not be prosecuted in a way that would avoid civilian deaths. The IRA might be able to reduce the number of such incidents, but not eliminate them completely. More IRA words would have to be found to try to get beyond the headlines and the embarrassment of this killing. At a time when Joanne Reilly's parents would have been placing her death notice, the IRA was working on a statement describing the bomb and what it thought had gone wrong; the cold mechanics and technology of war versus the human tears and horror of loss and death. And the 'human tragedy' was indeed immense – Joanne was just twenty. There is only one winner in that debate.

Years later, over a cup of coffee, I remember Colin Davidson's reaction of disbelief when I showed him the IRA statement of April 1989 – his sense of despair almost as he read those words. In the course of writing this book, I shared that statement with him again. I also sent him some of my news scripts from the time and asked for his thoughts. He sent me an immediate reaction: 'When you wrote your piece at 11 a.m., Paul and Anne Reilly probably didn't know that Joanne was dead. Lump in my throat. Knot in my stomach.' The following day, in a telephone conversation, he told me that the news scripts had taken him back 'to the terrifying bit'. Back in time. That morning in 1989, I was gathering information on the BBC news desk and writing radio scripts. My colleague Jane Dodge, now of Channel 4, was the reporter at the scene. All of this was in an era far removed from these modern times of communication. News was on the hour, not by the minute, and not by Twitter or Facebook. Those thirty-plus years ago, we were saved from those often instant and unthinking reactions.

Colin Davidson has thought about some words. They are a journey from my impersonal news scripts in the hours of the bomb into a very human and personal story; words that, today, stand tall as a kind and thoughtful expression of how the dead should be remembered. I have said it before and I repeat it here. Davidson paints with brushes and he paints with words:

Joanne Reilly would have been my age. I painted her father Paul in 2015, the sitting having taken place in her bedroom in their house in Warrenpoint. Paul had been a school caretaker and I remember him telling me of hearing the bomb explode: 'It sounded like a door closing,' he said. In so many ways, that's exactly what it was for Paul and his wife Anne. Every door closing, never to be reopened. For the rest of us, the sanitised news reports at the time told a familiar story of another so-called 'mistake'. Of someone being in the wrong place at the wrong time. But the fact is that Joanne was in the right place at the right time. She was in her place of work at 9.58 a.m. that morning. It was the human beings who drove that van and armed the device who were in the wrong place at the wrong time, as if they had a higher right to be there than Joanne. When I read the news notes now, I am transported to the bedroom in Warrenpoint, probably hastily left that morning in a rush to start a day's work. And I think of Paul, who heard a sound like a door closing.

These thirty-plus years later, Colin has given us the missing words from that day in April 1989. Three in particular: 'a door closing'. How remarkably simple, yet profound. A sound of war, of a news report – of that bomb, that day. Something the IRA should think about now. There were 150-plus words in the statement of explanation and 'sincerest apologies'. Yet that moment is captured in just three. That closing door – heard that day and, I am sure, on the many other days of the so-called mistakes. Part of an IRA truth could be to acknowledge the doors that were closed as the inevitable consequences of such actions.

The story of that period in the late 1980s can be summarised in a paragraph or two. Part of it is what I have just written about. The long list of civilian deaths is a confirmation of what Sir John Hermon described as both an inevitable and unavoidable part of the IRA campaign, not able to be brushed away or wished away in those words of deep regret and sincerest apologies. Words all too frequently drawn from the IRA dictionary. If there is to be anything that can be presented and described and possibly accepted as a republican 'truth', then they have to own this, state that the attacks were not 'mistakes' but part of their cold calculations of war, the collateral damage that I have described. Anything else is not worth saying, not worth repeating. It just digs us deeper into the lies of 'truth'.

At that time, the IRA was better armed and more active than it had been since the late 1970s. It was pressing attacks aimed at the army to make a point as that twentieth anniversary of the military presence approached in August 1989. The more it pressed, the more active it was, and the more obvious and open it became – at times, such as in Gibraltar, walking into the fire of the SAS. The longer the war, the fewer the surprises.

Yet, those talks had begun between Hume and Adams, and their parties. Fr Reid was involved. If not obvious at the time, it was the beginning of something. Then, late in 1989, the Northern Ireland Secretary of State Peter Brooke repeated a line on the IRA, that it was 'difficult to envisage a military defeat of such a force'. That comment, of course, led to another question, asked quietly at first and out of earshot: could the IRA defeat the British? We did not know it at the time, but soon, at arm's length and through a secret back-channel, the two sides would begin tentative contacts.

There was a military stalemate. Wars do not last forever. We see this more clearly from the vantage point of now. We did not see it then, as we were blinded by the actions of the IRA, the SAS and the loyalist organisations. Little was heard above the noise of the gunfire and explosions and the anger of condemnation. Yet, something was changing – hope hidden amongst the havoc and in the haemorrhaging of those times.

We were not allowed to see that hope. Those in the fight were not yet ready to share it. It was not seen in the UK government's military objective of 'the destruction of PIRA', or in an interview with the IRA leadership across several pages of *An Phoblacht* in August 1989. Under the headline 'We will break Britain's will', the IRA said: 'there will be no ceasefire and no truces until Britain declares its intent to withdraw and leave our people in peace'. That interview continued: 'We will, through inflicting continued and unsustainable losses, break the will of the British Government to stay in our country.' The lines of war are so easily scripted. Peace is a different proposition, an altogether more difficult challenge. It needs different pens, a new style of writing. It would take more time to find and to speak those different words – and then longer still to say them out loud.

But even as these tentative steps towards resolution were being taken, the North was faced with an escalating loyalist threat as the story of this place moved into the 1990s. And, between the lines of their many statements, there is a fear that is always present: that one day, or some day, they will be sold out. They were unsure who to trust, who to believe. It is the same thing we are hearing in 2022: Northern Ireland, the Union. They are not as certain as they once were – and there is a sense and mood in the unionist/loyalist community of losing.

# TWO

# Codewords and Coffee

*Meetings in 'the crucible'*

I HAVE DESCRIBED HOW SMALL this place is, how close we were to the war and it to us – too close at times. Talking across those different sides and lines brings you even closer. I exchanged contact details with numerous sources – a home number, a work number and perhaps some other number or place to leave a message. Back then, the immediate means of communication that we are so familiar with today – text, email and WhatsApp – did not exist. A mobile phone was not something you could slip into your back pocket.

I remember Val contacting me on one occasion. There had been a call to the home phone by someone looking for me – one of those nameless callers. Where might I be? It was urgent: 'This is the UFF, love.' As that loyalist killing surge escalated, these contacts and accompanying statements multiplied. I never had and never wanted to have pre-knowledge of intentions, but those statements, coming so soon after one attack and then the next, were written and delivered by those who knew. They would become a big part of my radio and television reporting in that period of the early 1990s. I remember a woman stopping to talk with me, telling me how the words 'Brian Rowan reports' always meant bad news. And another memory while walking in the street: two men passing, one saying to the other, 'That's your man who does all the murders.' This is an example of how close that war was. I had become one of the recognisable faces and voices reporting in that period of the conflict.

A new leadership was emerging. New weapons were available. And, for those deciding and directing the actions of the UDA and linked UFF, there was, in their thinking, a political reason and justification for escalating the violence. One statement warned that there would be an intensification 'to a ferocity never imagined'. I was watching and reporting on this killing surge, and met many times and in many places with the UDA leadership and those tasked with communicating on its behalf. In terms of its make-up, it was an open book – not a secret, all of them known. War seemed to be their full-time work. In numerous conversations, at all times of the day, I never heard any of them talk about their jobs. But they clearly had money, and enough of it to live well, if dangerously. In this period, I can't imagine that any of the insurance companies would have been rushing to write them a policy. Among them there were those who acted as if they were untouchable – one in particular. Perhaps he was. Perhaps they were. Perhaps they still are. Maybe some of them still know too much. That one in particular knows about the killing of the Belfast solicitor Pat Finucane – specific knowledge and information that has always been out of bounds.

My principal contact was a former Ulster Defence Regiment (UDR) soldier, who had morphed into a paramilitary 'brigadier', many ranks above his old station. He was one of those not-a-hair-out-of-place-type characters: dark hair, moustache, always dressed smart casual, never in a hurry. According to a senior loyalist source, he 'came from nowhere' into the highest ranks of the UDA. He no longer lives in Northern Ireland, but in exile – to this day persona non grata. I was in the room, on the Shankill Road, with journalist colleague Ivan Little in 1996, when the loyalist leadership dictated a statement to us, ordering him to leave, under threat. He stayed for a while, then realised he could stay no longer – not if he wanted to live. The statement was from the Combined Loyalist Military Command, an umbrella leadership of the UDA/UFF, UVF and Red Hand Commando, and tells one of the many stories of the power plays inside that world; why, for some, the wars are never over; why they always have to look back.

Before writing in detail on that significant period of the early 1990s, I want to explain the story of that emerging, new, loyalist leadership. It has its roots in the late 1980s, when, remarkably, the UDA was still legal and not yet on the list of proscribed organisations. Inexcusably, unforgivably, the systems – government, intelligence and security – acquiesced in the pretence of some difference or separation between the UDA and the UFF. There was none. Both lived under the same roof, looked into the same mirror. There were few who called out this scandal. In that period of the late 1980s, the organisation was turned upside down and inside out. In December 1987 one of its most prominent leaders, John McMichael, was killed by the IRA in an under-car bomb explosion. Then, just weeks later, another of its 'brigadiers', Davy Payne, was arrested and the UDA's share of a major arms consignment seized. I had met Payne once, in a drinking club in north Belfast. Andy Tyrie, the so-called 'supreme commander', had suggested I speak with him. This was sometime before his detention.

The guns of that arms shipment in the late 1980s would become loud and, to this day, remain loud in stories of agents and collusion. The arms were seized when Payne and others were arrested as part of a planned Special Branch operation. Cars that the loyalists were using had been tailed on their way to where the weapons were being held, but that tracking and following stopped short of the final destination. I was told that to follow any further on the roads they were travelling would have been much too obvious. So the police set up a road block and waited for the loyalists to make their return journey to Belfast.

The arms shipment had been organised through contacts in South Africa and came from the Lebanon. It was now in Northern Ireland and was to be split three ways between the UDA, UVF and Ulster Resistance. While UDA weapons were seized, many others were not. VZ58 rifles, Browning pistols, Bulgarian rocket launchers, Russian fragmentation grenades and ammunition that originated in China – all of these became the means and the making of that killing rage we were about to witness.

Many years later, I was told that Payne was not meant to move all of the UDA's share, but did so because the UVF was at the collection point at the same time and he feared that anything he left behind might be taken by them. At arranged meeting points, in Belfast and elsewhere, members from the different brigade areas of the UDA waited for Payne, waited for their guns, and waited longer than they expected. It was not until the news reports of the arms find and arrests that they learned of what went wrong. But the police operation had missed the central pick-up point in County Armagh; missed the UVF leaving with their weapons, as they travelled in a different direction from Payne; missed the weapons held by Ulster Resistance. It was this group, Resistance, that then resupplied or rearmed the UDA – something I reported thirty years ago, during my time at the BBC.

There are many questions still about that arms shipment; questions at the heart of the collusion argument. How, when there were so many agents – including at the top of the UDA – did the weapons get as far as Northern Ireland?* Brian Nelson, because of his role as an army agent, later became a headline. But he is only part of the picture; perhaps not even a

---

* Before I learned of the Special Branch operation which ended in UDA weapons being seized in 1988, another version of events had been outlined to me. That there was a breakdown in a surveillance operation as the arms were being shipped to Northern Ireland. This version of events was later dismissed by senior police sources.

big part in the manoeuvring in that critical phase of the arms deal in the latter part of the 1980s. At this point, Nelson was not as well informed as some might think. There were others, at a higher level of the loyalist leadership, who knew much more than he did. Yet there were so many gaps in intelligence. It is a story that does not add up. One of many such stories.

By March 1988 Andy Tyrie had been sacked, ousted in a vote of no confidence. Back then, I had been writing about the tensions and splits inside the UDA. I'd spoken to Tyrie and others, and had my first conversations with Jackie McDonald, McMichael's replacement on that 'brigadier' leadership. I heard the denials, the talking down of these suggestions of division. Then I was invited to the UDA headquarters at Gawn Street in east Belfast to talk about this. At the last minute, I was called by a colleague and advised not to go. I thought that I was going to see Tyrie but learned that he had invited others to be there. The intention was to question me about my sources and the stories I was hearing. I got someone to call Gawn Street and make my excuses. Then I started to worry, all part of figuring out how these worlds work and the wheels within them. Who to trust? Who to believe? Who knew what?

The following year – 1989 – the UDA itself, in an act of unbelievable arrogance, added its own piece to the wider collusion picture. This would contribute to the downfall of some of its long-established leaders.

On a Sunday in late August, I was contacted by a colleague. I was told that information would be made available to me at

the home of Tommy 'Tucker' Lyttle, then the UDA 'brigadier' in west Belfast, who lived in the heart of the Shankill.
There was a condition attached: that I could not report the
detail of how the information was made available to me,
and, instead, would have to say that I was taken away by the
UDA/UFF. I declined the UDA's offer, as did the journalist
who contacted me. The reason for saying no was the condition that had been applied. I would have been prepared to say
nothing about the source of the information. But this line and
the lie about being taken away by the UDA/UFF would have
walked me into too many questions from the police. It is not
hard to work out what they would have asked. Who made
the arrangements? How were they made? Where were you
picked up? What do you remember about the journey? What
were you shown? How many people in the room? How long
were you with them? Did you know them? Were you dropped
off where you were picked up? There would have been far too
many banana skins in that conversation.

The UDA wanted to share information, originating
from security forces, to 'prove' that one of its victims was
linked to the IRA. Within days, they found another way to
get the story out. In the fallout, UDA headquarters at Gawn
Street was raided. Then, within days, it emerged that documents were missing from Ballykinlar Army Camp and from
a police station in Belfast. The new RUC Chief Constable,
Hugh Annesley, called in an outside investigator. This was the
beginning of several collusion investigations headed by then
Cambridgeshire Deputy Chief Constable John Stevens (now

Lord Stevens), who would become the Metropolitan Police Commissioner. In the plays of these times, the UDA started wallpapering public places with security-force montages of republicans to show the quality of their targeting information. But the roof would cave in. They had gone too far. Loyalists blame Lyttle for what happened next – the raids and arrests that followed. 'Fucking stupid,' was how one former leader described Lyttle's actions. I was speaking with this source years later. 'I was trying to work it out,' he continued. I asked him if he thought that somebody was pulling Lyttle's strings? 'I do,' came the reply. 'I'd a question mark about him … I never trusted him and I never liked him.' I put it to him that Lyttle wasn't stupid. 'He was as stupid as a fox,' he replied, meaning not stupid at all. Yet, for the UDA, and for whoever thought it was a good idea, this turned out to be a monumental own-goal.

Brian Nelson, the army agent who ran the UDA's intelligence-gathering operation, was one of those arrested. His story, in all its detail and ugliness, for the army in particular, was about to come out of the bag. They are dead now, Nelson, Lyttle and Payne. Their stories gone with them, but not buried. There is much that can be pieced together. Part of the Lyttle story is told in the de Silva report[†] of December 2012, a review that examined the murder of Pat Finucane:

---

† In 2011, the British government stopped short of announcing a public inquiry into the murder of Belfast solicitor Pat Finucane. Sir Desmond de Silva QC carried out a review of the case.

'In my view Lyttle's links to some RUC officers during this period were so significant that they provided him with an entirely improper degree of protection and assistance in conducting his paramilitary activities as the brigadier for the west Belfast UDA.' It is a finding that shouts out about all that was wrong – the legal status of the UDA at this time and the far too cosy relationships that extended from such, some people thinking, believing, they were fighting on the same side.

It is out of the turmoil of that period in the late 1980s that the new loyalist leadership emerged and asserted itself.

As we moved into the early 1990s, the UDA was still using its UFF name as if it were some evil twin and somehow different. It would list its killings in statements delivered with the latest codewords to authenticate the information. Firstly, 'the Ulster Troubles', then 'the crucible'. From my notes, I can tell this change happened some time between late 1991 and early 1992. I wrote earlier that I was told of the change in a coffee meeting with one of the organisation's leaders not far from the BBC in Belfast. I wrote also that loyalists had given thought to this use of the term 'the crucible' to capture the intensity of the 'wars' at this time. Yet the man I met was always calm, never flustered; he walked and talked at an even pace. Those conversations could have been about anything – the weather, the football, what he would have for dinner later. The pulse rate rarely changed. Yet, he was there to discuss matters of life and death in a place of breakfasts and lunches and coffee and tea.

I often think back to those meetings, to my scribbling of notes, and wonder what the people a table or two away from us, or those behind the counter, were thinking. Did they have any idea of what was going on, the real purpose of these meetings? Were they interested? Were they listening? Or perhaps they were just too busy with other things to pay any attention to us, to stretch their ears to hear. These meetings happened out in the open, visible to others. In that sense they were not secret or private. Perhaps that was a good thing – no one would have thought or believed that such conversations would happen in a public place. Did I know everything about this man I was meeting? No. You never have all of the story. I had parts of it. Those parts were shared in meetings of this type and, at other times, in brief conversations on the phone. The duration of these was determined by how much change was in the telephone coin box – enough for a few seconds or for a couple of minutes.

It all seems so different now. It is crazy that those contacts were so routine and not at all out of the ordinary. For him, they were part of his war. For me, part of my work. Traffic in a two-way street. Too much traffic at times, too busy to find a quiet corner, and so it becomes part of the detailed thinking of now, how it all fits into those stories of our past and into those frames of truth.

I found another note from that period. I have it marked 1991. Full date unknown. But it's possibly from October that year. The RUC Chief Constable, Hugh Annesley, was speaking to me about changes in the UDA leadership:

It's perhaps, I suppose, topical to talk of the 'new guard' and the 'old guard'. I think there is very little doubt that the 'old guard', if you like, would have had a level of activity above which they would not have gone. And, I think, in that sense there was probably something of a restraining influence. I think that influence has now gone.

He continued:

I think that the team that are coming through are more aggressive … I think they are prepared to match some of the atrocities that PIRA have committed … and I think that some of those who might have stood in the way have been pushed to one side to be replaced by harder, more determined, more ruthless and better-quality individuals in their capacity to organise and carry out attacks within Northern Ireland.

McMichael was dead. Tyrie sacked. Payne and Lyttle in jail. Nelson, the army agent, was also in prison. Billy Elliot, another long-time leader in east Belfast, jumped before he was pushed. A younger leadership, including the former soldier who was to become my main point of contact with the UDA, was now in place with the tools of war available to them.

The script of these times is not just about that new leadership and those guns and the graphs that, over time, would show the UFF and the UVF first match and then exceed the killing rate of the IRA. There was more to the loyalist story – more about politics in their statements; a joining up of the various organisations in that Combined Loyalist Military Command. Then there was a conditional ceasefire to coincide with political talks in 1991 – different thinking and different words in this phase of the loyalist war; words that were unexpected and words that made us stop and think, because they interrupted the routine and the ways of that time.

The backdrop to the loyalist statement announcing a conditional ceasefire was the 'usual', the constant of violence, including 'spectacular' headlines, such as when the IRA launched mortar bombs at Downing Street, where Prime Minister John Major was present. A splash headline in *An Phoblacht* on 14 February 1991 shouted: 'IRA bombs War Cabinet'. Inside the republican newspaper and across a couple of pages, there was another headline: '"We remain totally committed and confident in victory" – Óglaigh na hÉireann'. This attack, in the period of the Gulf War, had happened a week earlier, on 7 February 1991. The Gulf crisis meant all eyes were on developments there and, in that period, the IRA used the opportunity to make its own headlines. *The Independent* reported:

The IRA yesterday breached high war-time security surrounding the core buildings of British government to fire three home-made mortar bombs across White-hall in broad daylight, one exploding only 15 yards from the 10 Downing Street room where the War Cabinet was sitting. It is the closest the Provisionals have come to murdering the Prime Minister and other senior Cabinet members since the Brighton bombing in 1984, when five people died and 30 were injured.

Across the newspapers, a significant part of the coverage concentrated on the blindness of the intelligence agencies; how they failed to see any of the preparations for this attack. Their eyes were elsewhere, looking at other things.

Back in Northern Ireland, loyalists were in that high-tempo phase of activity, including a UVF attack in which four men were shot dead in Cappagh, County Tyrone. Three were IRA members: John Quinn (23), Malcolm Nugent (20) and Dwayne O'Donnell (17). They were in a car outside a pub. The fourth victim, fifty-two-year-old Thomas Armstrong, was killed when shots were fired through a window into the bar. I was in Cappagh that night. I heard the anger. It was not long before the talk of collusion became loud again. In this climate, there was nothing to suggest that a ceasefire, even of some conditional nature, was possible. Not now, not in this atmosphere. Yet, away from the headlines in London and here, loyalists were shaping this most unlikely and unexpected of initiatives. Alongside the killing, in this hell before the calm, a discussion about politics was also happening, quietly, at this time – it was not something we knew about or understood just yet. In the background, a different conversation was beginning to happen that would eventually produce a more public loyalism in the faces and voices of Gusty Spence, David Ervine, William 'Plum' Smith, Billy Hutchinson, Gary McMichael, Davy Adams and Ray Smallwoods. But, for now, that conversation was happening out of our vision and out of our earshot.

Something was changing and, in an early expression of this, we would read the terms of the conditional ceasefire of 1991 in a statement of twenty-eight lines. This was the first statement under that new heading of Combined Loyalist Military Command. I was one of three journalists invited to the headquarters of the UDA in east Belfast on 17 April that year. The others were Ivan Little and Alan Murray. My principal UDA contact, the former soldier, was there, now firmly established not just in the leadership of this organisation, its so-called 'inner council', but in that wider Combined Command. There was a second representative of the UDA leadership present, one of the few older men to survive the purge of the late 1980s. Two senior members of the UVF were also in the room, one of them the late Jim McDonald, who, a few years later, would have a seat at the loyalist top table when the ceasefires of 1994 came to be announced. But there was a long road yet to travel from 1991 and from this initial suspension of violence to the historic developments of 1994, which would open up wider possibilities in terms of peace and political agreements and place loyalism on a different stage.

Earlier, I wrote about violence being part of the negotiation of peace. We can better understand now how loyalists would have seen themselves in positions of advantage and strength at this time; why, in 1991, they would have considered this as a moment to get a step ahead of the IRA, by stepping back to allow a breathing space for political dialogue, talks that would involve some, but not all. The ceasefire statement was written in conditional terms. Of course, it had to be at this time. There would be a 'universal suspension of aggressive operational hostilities'. It would begin at midnight on the eve of political talks. Loyalists expected no change from the IRA: 'So let them therefore be warned that the Combined Command will order defensive and, where fitting, retaliatory action if so required. Such action will be extremely discriminatory and to grave effect.' This final sentence was in bold type and underlined.

The date was 17 April 1991. There were thirteen more days on the calendar before those political talks would begin. And we would quickly learn that before those talks there would be no change to the rules. Within hours of the statement being made, the UFF shot dead a taxi driver. The 'suspension of aggressive operational hostilities' would not begin until midnight on 29 April and would end at midnight on 4 July. And within that period the UFF shot dead a Sinn Féin councillor, Eddie Fullerton, in County Donegal, and the UVF shot and wounded a republican in north Belfast. These shootings were, in their terms, part of the 'retaliatory action' they had threatened.

The conditional loyalist ceasefire, and the political talks of that time, were ignored by the IRA. Indeed, in some of its actions, the IRA appeared to be attempting to goad the loyalist organisations. And it was always the intention of those groups within the Combined Command to step out of ceasefire when the political talks ended; to return to their wars and to their codewords, to the battlefields of Ulster's unfinished business.

There were so many statements in that time, among them those I recall because of other things that were happening, such as hearing of a loyalist shooting at the Devenish Arms in December 1991 as I was leaving a meeting with the IRA, represented by a man and a woman in balaclavas, in an upstairs room of a house in west Belfast. Another man, a republican who brought me there, sat on the bedroom floor throughout. The briefing I was given there was part of my preparation for a wider report I was compiling for the BBC for use in early January 1992. It was an analysis of the IRA that would include the background thinking of the then Army General in Northern Ireland, Sir John Wilsey, and the RUC's Special Branch. There were also interviews with Martin McGuinness, the priest Fr Denis Faul and the Social Democratic and Labour Party (SDLP) deputy leader Seamus Mallon. None of those men are with us now. They're no longer here to comment on the wars and the peace of this place.

Aidan Wallace, who was twenty-two, was shot dead in that gun attack at the Devenish Arms, just three days before Christmas. The loyalist statement on the attack was part of the cycle and the routine that had become the bloody normal of this place. Just another day. And I recall another statement, in February 1992, after gunmen fired forty-seven shots inside a bookmaker's shop in the lower Ormeau Road in south Belfast. It was a day and a statement I revisited in a piece of writing for the *Belfast Telegraph* twenty years later, in February 2012. This is some of what I wrote:

> In the rushed delivery of the loyalist statement, the newsroom typist thought she had heard the words 'Remember Strabane'. The telephone call to the BBC was more than 20 years ago; the anonymous caller representing the UDA. He was dictating a statement after the gun attack on a bookies' shop on the Ormeau Road, an attack in which five people were killed. It came within weeks of the IRA slaughter of eight workmen, travelling home in a minibus, targeted in a bomb explosion at Teebane. And it was that attack that the UDA tried to use as justification for the bookmaker's shootings. The closing words of its statement, delivered with the codeword 'crucible', should have read 'Remember Teebane'. In a conflict stretching across decades, there were many such statements from one organisation and then another. These were the words of explanation and attempted justification delivered after the bombs and the bullets. All sorts of spurious allegations were made in that UDA statement 20 years ago; lies now exposed in a recent television interview given by one of the organisation's leaders, Jackie McDonald. He was in jail in 1992 when

the shootings happened, but he knows they were part of a retaliation 'numbers-game' in which 'innocent people usually suffer'. I asked McDonald if the people in the bookies were innocent, to which he replied: 'Of course.' 'If there had been a war between loyalism and republicanism, I'd have rather seen them taking the war to each other, not to the communities. But that's where it took everybody.' I then asked him, was it too hard to say sorry? 'I can't say sorry, because I wasn't part of it.' He means in 1992, when some other paramilitary 'brigadier' will have been in charge; in this case, the man who came up with the codeword 'crucible'.

These days never stay in their time. They are a continuous story, always evolving. Questions develop with knowledge. In 2022, more pages were added to those days in 1991 and 1992. A report by the Police Ombudsman outlined the findings of an investigation that included those killings in the bookies' shop and the murder of Aidan Wallace; an investigation that examined the role of informers inside the UDA in south Belfast – their information, what happened and did not happen, as well as significant investigative and intelligence failures, and 'collusive behaviours'. These findings by the Police Ombudsman read back into the days of the RUC.

Those killings are in that time and in that period defined by those words 'the crucible'. The former UDR soldier who spoke for the collective UDA/UFF leadership at that time was the organisation's south Belfast 'brigadier' – the man who was in charge when McDonald was in jail. It was in that part of the city, on the Lisburn Road, sometimes close to the BBC and on the Taughmonagh estate, that I would often meet him. I called him on 5 February 1992 to clarify the closing words in that rushed statement not long after those bullets were fired inside the bookies' shop. What are the missing parts in his story – this man of casual conversations and those words, 'the crucible'? Where does he fit within that 2022 report by the Police Ombudsman? Thirty years previously, he had the rank to give orders and would have had detailed knowledge in relation to that series of killings.

These stories never end. That man, now in exile, is not likely to answer any questions – more silent, more careful, in the peace than he was in the war, with more to worry about now than he did then. I know from a comment, made by a senior police officer, that the RUC knew that I was meeting with him at that time back in the 1990s; part of how close and how regular such contacts became in my reporting of that war – part of what became 'normal'. Something that still makes me think now.

On 6 February, the mood of 1992 was summarised in eighteen words across the top of page 2 of *The Independent*: 'Seasoned observers speak of a sense of hopelessness; of misery piled on misery; of a community in shock.' We were waiting for what would happen next. A waiting that means you almost immediately lose touch with what has just happened. That hopelessness means that there is no time to dwell in the present, but rather you prepare yourself or get ready for those next actions and words. The day after the bookies' attack, I interviewed one of the leaders of the UDA, who spoke of the recent IRA violence and how, in that context, he could 'understand' why the shootings had happened:

> UDA leader: As far as I can understand, if the campaign of genocide that the Provisional IRA carry out on the Protestant/loyalist community, if that was to cease tomorrow, I couldn't see the circumstances in which the Ulster Freedom Fighters would carry out attacks anywhere.

> Rowan: You're saying basically that it's your belief that if IRA republican violence ceases, then the likelihood arises that loyalist violence would also cease.

> UDA leader: I would go along with that.

Those words, in that interview with the BBC, became part of the newspaper coverage the next day. Calls for the UDA to be banned were loud. Such a move was still months away, but would happen in 1992, without denting its killing capacity. There was also a slow realisation that talks that excluded republicans and loyalists would always come up short; that there is a difference between a political agreement and a peace agreement. The IRA could not be wished away, condemned away. This would become the Hume argument for inclusive negotiations – a penny that would take more time to drop when there was no such time to spare.

In a Zoom conference in 2022, I commented that I no longer hear John Hume's voice in our politics, meaning the learning that he left behind. It is often referenced, but rarely practised. Hume stepped above party politics and rivalries to a height where he could see what needed to happen and find a corridor out of conflict. He was a leader. A visionary. Listen today to some of the commentary on the war. There are those who talk about it even though they have little or no experience of it. If they are not careful, they may repeat the mistakes of the past, rather than learn the lessons of Hume.

# THREE

# Dark Glasses and Tape

## *Bodies on the Border*

'A THIRD PARTY WAS ENGAGED to invite two journalists to meet with representatives of the Army [the IRA]. They were invited to a rendezvous.' Those words were given to me in January 2022, by a former P. O'Neill. They take me back to some thirty years previously – to July 1992. The arrangements then were not by one of those RSVP-type invitations. There was no card in the post; no name or address; no date by which to respond; nothing of that kind – but something much more anonymous and secretive. Somewhere along some road, the IRA was waiting for us. We had not been told the estimated time of the journey. In fact, we had been told nothing. I was in a car, tape across my eyes, with dark glasses over the tape. My journalist colleague Eamonn Mallie was beside me on the back seat. His eyes were also covered. I was glad he was there. I told him so. In that moment, in that situation, I was grateful for his company – grateful, even though we work in a business that is about being first and about exclusives.

There were two men in the front. Someone we knew had linked us up with them, but, in the way of these things, there had been no introductions. In these plays, the actors don't have names. The backdrop to this journey was the story of the discovery of the remains of a young woman, Margaret Perry, and, elsewhere, there were three bodies on the border. I was still trying to process all of that – and now I had something more to think about, this rendezvous with the IRA.

The night before, I had been with a BBC camera and sound crew that had come across two of those bodies. What was about to happen next was the telling of the story in the words of the IRA. That is why we were in the car, on another road to somewhere behind the scenes of war. What if we were stopped at a security checkpoint? Back then, it could so easily have happened. What was our explanation? There wasn't one – nothing that would be remotely credible or believable. There would be no way of talking ourselves out of that situation, no easy answers. The tape and the glasses, and the strangers in the front seats without tape and glasses, would be hard to explain. So the only option would have been silence: to say nothing; take our medicine, whatever that would be. These are the thoughts that raced and, on occasions, still race through my head – all part of trying to navigate an impossible road. How mad it seems now. What a crazy place we lived in.

I remember, years later, our daughter Elle listening to the story and looking at me almost in disbelief. She heard it alongside another story that Mervyn Jess was telling. Jess had reported from the scenes of many killings – at La Mon, Darkley, Enniskillen, Loughgall, the Docklands bomb in London, and Omagh, as well as from Iraq and Afghanistan – but, well into the peace now, he was working on something for television about the oldest identical twins in the UK, Dot and Daisy. Then I told the story of the tape and glasses and the bodies on the border. Elle, and others in our company, out on a Saturday afternoon for a drink and some lunch, were then made to think about that other planet that once was this place.

Fortunately, the car was not stopped at any checkpoint. We arrived at a house. Our eyes were still taped until we got upstairs. We were brought in one at a time, then frisked before being told we could remove the tape. We were in a room with two men, their faces hidden behind balaclavas. They had a long statement to read, written on toilet paper, to be flushed away quickly if there were any problems. It would take what felt like a longer time to write it down: words that would explain how the remains of the young woman came to be found buried in woods; how she was killed; who killed her; why they killed her. The statement would also detail the execution of three IRA men after interrogation: Gregory Burns, Aidan Starrs and John Dignam. It was a story about the enemy within: how these men were turned and used, what happens when you are found out. And it was a story with lines about handlers, payments and plots, and about Special Branch and MI5. The bodies on the border were there as a warning to others – that there is no hiding place, no forgiveness, not in these cases, not when you have betrayed your own.

My news reports at the time were mechanical. In a sequence of developments, I reported that, firstly, the IRA had issued a statement to *The Irish News* in Belfast, which said the location of the body of a missing woman had been established. The reading between the lines of this statement was that informers or agents had played a part in the woman's death. Margaret Perry had been missing for a little over a year. By the following morning, the news had moved on to the three bodies on the border. I had been to south Armagh. My news scripts included the following: that just outside the village of Newtownhamilton on the road to Dundalk, a naked body had been dumped on a grass verge; elsewhere, on the short stretch of road between Crossmaglen and Cullaville, another body lay under a black plastic sheet with a milk crate set on top. Here, I said, the security forces were keeping a watch from close by. And it was understood that the third body had been left in the area of Belleeks. The men whose bodies they were had been put through a self-styled IRA court martial and shot. All of this was before that meeting with the IRA. That invitation had not yet been issued. The eventual meeting was still some hours away.

In actual time, you get on with it – hide behind the news. There is no time to think, other than about the circumstances and the predicaments of that moment. There are immediate things to worry about, such as those I outlined earlier. What if we were stopped? We knew we were completely compromised. It was obvious we were with the IRA – too obvious. Then, being in the house with these men in balaclavas – what if there was a raid? What would we say? Again, silence would have been the only option. This play that had been created by the IRA was the complete opposite of the types of meeting I described earlier with my principal UDA contact. So why did it have to be like that?

Thirty years on, I decided to revisit that day. I met and spoke with the man who had issued that invitation through a third party. I met him to hear his side of the story. Why the arrangements had to be as they were. What the thinking was inside his head on that summer day of 1992. The first of two meetings was in late January 2022. It was like being back in time. First a walk, my phone switched off. Then, sitting on a bench; pauses in the conversation as people walked by; me explaining to him what I was trying to do in this book; my questions about the tape, the glasses, the car, the house and that long briefing that I had copied down in the company of the IRA those thirty years previously. That night my source called me. He said he had the book I had asked to borrow. I could collect it when I was ready. This was his way of saying that he had the answers for me. So, the next morning, we met again. His answers were handwritten, in block capitals, half an A4 page. Some of the detail of those long-ago events was dealt with in twenty-six lines. Information in 2022 was as controlled as it had been in 1992.

The new information shared with me revealed that the statement of 1992, that long briefing, had been 'drafted the day before their execution' – meaning the day before Dignam, Starrs and Burns were shot by the IRA. There had been 'careful consideration of all the revelations made during their interrogation'; consideration, also, of how 'the issue of M' (a reference to Margaret Perry) was handled. I understand that one of those being held by the IRA thirty years earlier was taken away from that interrogation, that court martial, to pinpoint her grave. Then a priest was contacted with the details of the location of the body. The IRA was managing and sequencing events. That handwritten note of 2022 tells me that thirty years earlier, when drafted, the statement on Dignam, Starrs and Burns 'was taken to the CS for clearance'. 'CS' means IRA chief of staff, a position held then by the late Kevin McKenna. His name does not appear in the handwritten twenty-six lines given to me in January 2022. But from other sources, I know that in 1992 he held that position on the IRA Army Council. McKenna died in 2019. Gerry Adams gave the oration.

'In considering the release of the statement, it was decided to do so by way of a briefing of journalists … A third party was engaged to invite two journalists to meet with representatives of the Army [the IRA]. They were invited to a rendezvous.' I'm reading the January 2022 note. Back again in that moment and that predicament of thirty years previously:

Arrangements had been made for volunteers to pick them up from the arranged location. They were to be made to wear plasters over their eyes and to don glasses as covering. Their route to the premises where they would meet two volunteers was well-scouted, and [the possibility of] interception was extremely minimal. The Army [the IRA] was aware that these precautions would be severe and discomfiting for the journalists involved. They were considered necessary given the gravity of the situation.

When I read the words, I am back in time, remembering those men joining our company – the 'volunteers'. How functional it was, being told to put the glasses on, being guided outside towards the car. I have a memory of my arm being held at times, perhaps as we approached a step. And then a journey of not many words. Thirty years on, that word 'discomfiting' jumps out from those twenty-six lines. Is that how I felt? I checked its meaning, what the dictionary says: to make someone feel uneasy or embarrassed. Thirty years ago, it was all of that and some more. I wasn't so much embarrassed. We were doing our work, on this occasion, in a way determined by others. It was out of our control. Uneasy, yes. Nervous, yes – because of circumstances that could not be explained away if that car was intercepted.

The note of 2022 describes the men who were executed as 'intelligence assets'. 'The need for protection of the Army [the IRA] and the journalists, given the context, was of paramount importance.' This is the last sentence in the note – the line, that takes us back to IRA thinking those thirty years previously, and explains the tape and glasses and all the other steps in preparation for that meeting. Did it have to be done that way? The IRA, at that time, in their war, believed there was no other way.

My television news report that evening in July 1992 tells nothing of the back story, not as I knew it then and better understand it now. Nothing about the tape and glasses; nothing about the men in the car; nothing about the questions that raced through my head those few hours earlier; nothing about the house and the men in balaclavas; nothing about being searched before that long statement was read and we wrote it down in the presence of the IRA; then putting the tape and the glasses back on, being taken back to the car and being dropped off where we had been picked up. Left then with all of that swimming in our heads, information becomes a swamp, holds you down. I knew we would have left the goggles or glasses in the car, but I couldn't remember what I did with the tape, whether we were asked to leave that also, or whether I just binned it. I have since been told that it was 'retained' by the IRA.

Then it was back to the BBC to explain all of this to a number of editors and decide what to do with the detail we had; how to think straight in that moment, when there was every reason to be disorientated. The introduction to my report that evening read: 'In a statement this afternoon the IRA has given details of the alleged roles the three men had with the intelligence services.' Factually correct, of course, but not the story of that day – not even close. When I got home, I wept. Cried as I told the story to Val. There was no news to hide behind now. None of those immediate questions and worries relating to the car journey and the meeting in the house, which, in actual time, serve as a shield and a distraction. It was different now. There was just a lot to think about after a not-so-ordinary day at the office: the shock of seeing the bodies; how they had been left; the nature of that meeting with the IRA, the explanations after the executions. This, within hours of each other. Now, when I reflect, I realise how sick this place had become – that illness. Coming to live with it, accepting it, treating it as normal, refusing help – of course, I want those days to go away, but in all of their detail, they stay with me. How mad and bizarre and crazy it all seems now.

The next day, in conversation with one of the BBC editors, Tom Kelly (who went on to be a spokesman for Mo Mowlam, Peter Mandelson and then Tony Blair), I was offered some counselling. I declined. Probably, in those times, I thought it might suggest some weakness, that there was something 'wrong' with me. I know now that there was something wrong, of course there was. But thirty years ago, this was stuff we tried to blank out, without ever being able to throw it out. Recently, I called Tom to get his memory of that moment. He said it 'wasn't a formal offer' but him 'recognising the traumatic nature of the event'. He also remembered that the late Paddy O'Flaherty, veteran radio reporter, had been at that scene in south Armagh too and that the bodies that had been dumped were naked: 'There was something in your face and something in Paddy's face that made me recognise that even for experienced reporters this was qualitatively different. It was a new level of horror.'

I think I know what Tom means when he speaks about 'a new level of horror'. For me, that 'new' was being taken so close to it all – to those bodies, to the balaclavas, to the words that knew exactly how these men died – and how the remains of Margaret Perry were found. It was so close that I could think inside those IRA interrogations; the questioning of Dignam, Starrs and Burns; their answers; their fate. Thinking about tape and glasses and that journey, and how news changes you, it was something not properly recognised then, but fully understood now.

It took me something like ten years, long after the cease-fires, to allow myself to begin to tell some of that story. Firstly, in a few lines of writing, and then, over a period of time, I started talking about it in public events, such as festival conversations. The first time I did so, you could have heard a pin drop. I was in the Falls Road Library in west Belfast being interviewed as part of Féile an Phobail. It was 2008.

I still think many times about that day and that meeting in July 1992, about the things that were missing from the news reports then, such as the opening words from the IRA in that meeting behind the scenes of war, in some house, somewhere: 'We have brought you here this afternoon to deal with the executions of Gregory Burns, Aidan Starrs and John Dignam. I will read a briefing and then answer questions.' P. O'Neill was speaking thirty years ago. His words were delivered as matters of fact. But they were and are one side of a story, with details that, no doubt, others would dispute and challenge. The words were cold, as cold as those bodies that were dumped on those border roads:

> The three who have been executed are Gregory Burns, a British Intelligence agent since 1979, and RUC informers John Dignam and Aidan Starrs. All three were IRA volunteers who have been under suspension ... Last week, with our enquiries complete, our volunteers arrested Burns, Dignam and Starrs and, in the course of courts martial, the three made full confessions of their activities, including their part in the disappearance and brutal murder of Portadown woman Margaret Perry.

In that IRA briefing in 1992, we were told how Burns, Dignam and Starrs had been 'suspended from the IRA pending full investigations into allegations of corruption'. That briefing also described a 'relationship' between Burns and Margaret Perry, which Burns ended. It stated how Burns and Starrs feared Margaret Perry could expose them to the IRA. This seems to be a reference to the alleged 'corruption' or criminality they were involved in. Did she know of Burns' involvement with the military? I don't know. The briefing then detailed how Starrs killed Margaret Perry and how she was disappeared, details I will not record here. There is a line in the briefing about how Starrs later returned to the murder scene to remove evidence. This time, according to the IRA, he was accompanied by Dignam. As the briefing continued, the IRA then claimed that Special Branch recruited Dignam and Starrs after the murder. These lines in the briefing take us into the dirty war – into those rooms where people break and are turned; to what is ignored because of some higher intelligence need. How important information was. How unimportant some lives were. In a conversation in 2022, a one-time senior IRA figure described Margaret Perry as 'the only innocent in the story'.

We don't know who interrogated Dignam, Starrs and Burns. There has been reporting that it may have been 'Stakeknife', a British Army agent operating inside IRA internal security. I am told that is not the case; that, two years previously, he had been stood down after security forces raided a house where another suspected informant was being questioned. This whole area of agents or informants or sources, how they were run, how they were discarded or found out, is one of the ugliest chapters in the 'dirty war'. A story of many shadows and of many ghosts.

I often think about the eeriness of the border that night in July 1992 – the dark, how quiet it was, that moment of being there with the dead. I have thought many times since about what I think I would do if I came across a body in normal circumstances, outside that context; that I would call for help, perhaps say a prayer; that I would stay there, at least until someone else arrived. I would do something, but not that night. The bodies became pictures and news. I remember as we approached the scene where one of the bodies was covered with black plastic sheeting, there were voices from behind us. In the still of that night and that moment, they were voices from nowhere; shouts from a hedge. It took some working out. Soldiers were watching from nearby, warning us to get away. On occasion, booby-trap bombs are placed at these scenes, hoping to catch the security forces in follow-up operations. The area had not yet been checked and cleared. It was too early for that to have happened. The BBC war correspondent Kate Adie was at the scene. 'The hedge spoke,' she recalled. And when she heard the words 'Fuck off ma'am', she knew it was the army. I remember how things calmed when the soldiers realised it was her.

After that it was back to the BBC to write and record the early-morning news scripts – those mechanical, impersonal accounts of those hours. I think I then went home for a short while, before I took that call with its detail of a meeting place in Belfast. Eamonn Mallie was there, and someone else whom we both knew. He waited with us until the IRA arrived. It was then that Mallie and I were given the dark glasses, guided towards a car and given the tape to put across our eyes. At this point, others had taken control of events. We had been handed over to them. It would not happen that way again; not with this organisation; not with all that intrigue in the shadows.

Mallie and I would later meet with the man who linked us up with the IRA on that occasion to explain why it could not happen that way again, that in such circumstances we were completely compromised. We got away with it on that occasion. But it could so easily have been very different; would have been very different and difficult had that car been stopped by the army or the police. Mallie and I, certainly in that period, stuck out like sore thumbs. We were well known. I have often made the point that we are not foreign correspondents sent to report on war situations. We live here. We are emotionally attached – stitched into the fabric. We live in the death of this place; live with the experiences of that day and many others; live with the knowledge of what we can say and cannot say; live with the ghosts. And all of that lives inside what I call the mind's wardrobe – still there when you open the door.

I read in the *Lost Lives* book, one of the tallest pillars of journalistic work spanning the conflict and peace periods, that Aidan Starrs' father told the inquest that although his son had not returned home after visiting the republican commemoration at Bodenstown, he had no suspicion that anything was wrong. That commemoration was just days before the bodies were dumped on the border, those scenes a reminder of the ugliness and the brutality and the penalties of war. Yet, there was something said in Bodenstown, in June 1992, that made us pay attention, made us think closely about those words delivered by the Belfast republican Jim Gibney – different words, words that were heard in the loyalist community, words some considered worth further exploration. Indeed, some interpreted the speech as the flying of a kind of peace kite: 'Some years ago at an internal Sinn Féin education seminar in Derry, I picked up a telling phrase from a member of the Protestant community who, very bravely, took the step of addressing us,' Gibney said. 'He talked about attitudes within the Protestant community towards us and he said that our appeals to them can't be heard above the "deadly sound of gunfire"'. Then, some lines later in the speech, Gibney asked if republicans had been deafened by the 'deadly sound of their own gunfire'. This extract followed:

> We know and accept that the British government's departure must be preceded by a sustained period of peace and will arise out of negotiations. We know and accept that such negotiations will involve the different shades of Irish nationalism and Irish unionism engaging the British government either together or separately to secure an all-embracing and durable peace process. We know and accept that this is not 1921 and that at this stage we don't represent a government in waiting. We're not standing in the airport lounge waiting to be flown to Chequers or Lancaster House; we have no illusions of grandeur. Idealists we are, fools we are not.

I think about what we could not see then, but what has developed since, some of it very quickly: the IRA ceasefires of 1994 and 1997; the historic political agreement of 1998; then, through to today, the remarkable rise of Sinn Féin north and south and the louder debate about a 'New Ireland'. That term, 'New Ireland', was used in the Gibney speech all those years ago. There was a vision and, I suppose, a prediction, in those words of 1992 that could only be properly understood if, like Gibney, you were on the inside of this thinking and talking that was happening on some other stage.

I mentioned that those thirty years ago, loyalists were trying to read the signals and read the signs. Some were more willing than others to test the possibilities in this script; to try to read through, or to see through, to what might be on the next pages. The UVF said the 'next logical step' was for Sinn Féin to persuade the IRA to cease its violence, 'which in turn will bring a positive response from this source'. The UDA, however, was much more cautious and caustic: 'We believe that until they, the republican sectarian murder gangs, desist from their murderous campaign, we cannot on behalf of our organisation and the communities from which our volunteers are enlisted, make any response which would give these republican groups any vestige of credibility ...' Within weeks, the UDA was proscribed, ending one of the scandals of the conflict period; a recognition, at last, that there was no real difference between the UFF and its front organisation. Then, as we turned into 1993, the gunfire got louder. It deafened us all. The road to peace would be through another hell; stepping over more bodies; more convulsions before the calm. The UK government was communicating with the republican leadership – with Martin McGuinness and Gerry Kelly – interpreted by many as talking to the IRA, talking to the enemy and steps towards some sort of sell-out.

# FOUR

# The Hell before the Calm

*'John Hume, Gerry Adams and the nationalist electorate will pay a heavy, heavy price'*

WE HAD NO IDEA WHAT we were looking at; could see it only as a rising body count – conflict stuck in the mechanics and the machinations and the manoeuvres of war. Things were getting worse, more worrying. There was nothing in the windows of those times to suggest a wind of change. In the circumstances of then, talk of peace seemed such an odd notion. Those much more overt actions and statements of war still dominated the space and the narrative. Yet we know now that what we were seeing was the most unlikely beginnings of some end; at last, some way out of our darkness.

There were moments in 1993 when the heat in 'the crucible' became unbearable; when the security assessment that things were not out of control sounded so utterly ridiculous. It was a year when the IRA offered the UK government a choice – peace talks or the inevitability of more war; the year when the latest phase of the Hume–Adams talks became public. Then, in October, there was the IRA Shankill bomb and what happened afterwards, foreshadowed in a statement from the UFF, its words telephoned to the BBC just hours after the explosion, threatening 'a heavy price' for the attack. The year reads like a crisis calendar that also covers the dates of another loyalist attempt to smuggle a huge arms shipment into Northern Ireland and then the breaking of one particular story in the biggest headlines – a story that told of secret contacts between the British government and the IRA. Already, this place was a nervous wreck, needing all the medication and treatments and therapies that were available. At times, it was unable to cope – people hiding, not wanting to come out the door. How would Northern Ireland, or the North, survive? How could it survive? There were moments when I thought we were going over the edge.

There had been a build-up to that madness of 1993. Over a period of time, we had recognised this sharper edge to the loyalist war. Part of it was a more focused targeting of Sinn Féin and, at times, attacks on the homes and offices of members of the SDLP. We know now that in all of this we were watching the loyalist organisations trying to shoot and bomb their way out of the fears they had: the constant sense of siege and sell-out; not trusting the British government; believing they could be betrayed; always needing reassurance; not having enough shoulders to look over. Their statements were their words of anger; their next last stand. Prepared for peace, but ready for more war. I heard it all, read it all. Cross words at another of Ulster's crossroads. Life and death in 'the crucible'. I had so many meetings with those loyalists – at times, just after they had met as an 'inner council', all of them in the room. Me there to hear their statements, read their statements, report their statements and read their minds – that open book that told their story.

This was the year when the Shankill loyalist Johnny Adair joined that 'inner council' leadership as west Belfast 'brigadier'. There was nothing anonymous about him, nothing shy or secret. His name was all over the place, on the tip of every tongue. He had an ego the size of his rank. He's another of that leadership now in exile – someone else who had to run. Belfast, a city he once terrorised, is too dangerous for him now. Back in the early 1990s, did he change the loyalist war? Was he a significant player in that escalation? The answer to both questions is yes. He was in the engine room, shovelling coal onto the many fires; making the hell of those times. In one conversation with me, he described a ladder on which they had hit Sinn Féin up and down its rungs – in the ranks at the bottom, in the middle and at the top. In 1993 I started to write his obituary, believing he would not survive. He was too open, too public, too onstage, such a big target.

In March that year, I met him in his home of bulletproof glass, reinforced doors and steel shutters. He wore body armour and spoke off-camera, not wanting his face on television – he'd already had a close shave. I think this was his first interview since then. Just days earlier, the IRA had attempted to kill him on the streets of the Shankill. The sound of those bullets would still have been ringing in his ears. As his story developed, Adair would become the loyalist equivalent of the cat with nine lives. He would need them all.

Just weeks later, I was interviewing him again, after an undercover soldier, involved in a surveillance operation at his home, fired shots at Adair and two of his friends. One of them was grazed by a bullet. The other two were uninjured. They had challenged the soldier on the street; challenged the wrong person – someone who was ready for them. That night, Adair had someone call me – a woman. It was late. The message: 'Johnny wants to see you.' I remember stepping into Hazelfield Street. Alone. It was dark and I was lit up by the security light on his home. I nearly jumped out of my skin at the next sound. Then I realised what it was. The rattle of the steel shutter behind his front door. Inside, the house was busy, noisy. A number of men were sitting at a table to my left. Someone else was coming down the stairs. It seemed there was a lot going on. I knew not to ask. Better not to know. Gina Adair asked would I like a coffee. I said, 'No thanks.' As we were discussing what had happened earlier, her husband spoke of being under '24-hour surveillance' and said he believed that British Intelligence was waiting for him to make a mistake so they could kill him.

In September 1993 the IRA tried again, but the plan failed. Once more, Adair was in contact, or someone called me on his behalf. I cannot recall the precise detail. I do remember travelling up to the Shankill with a cameraman and another reporter. They waited in the car until I found out what was happening. Adair met me on the street. It was a charades-type moment – all actions, no words. I worked it out. He wanted to know where the camera was. I went back to the car and told them to head back to the office. I knew enough to know we were being walked into a stunt of some description.

Later, a photograph emerged of masked gunmen at a makeshift barrier, with a message that the UFF would police the streets. The IRA spoke of an absolute determination to make Adair 'pay for his crimes'. He was inside their heads, inside their plans. They were chasing him, hunting him. And it was this fascination with him, that absolute determination to kill him, that led to the unthinking madness of the Shankill bomb.

Perhaps jail saved Adair from those who wanted him dead. Before the ceasefires of 1994, he was in prison, as was the former UDR soldier who had been my key link to that loyalist leadership. Both were as influential inside as they were outside – their support and votes would be needed if anything was to change.

Was there some way out of the mayhem and the madness of those times? Not yet, but Hume and Adams were trying to find one. In the condemnation of their talks, this was missed. For many, there is a strange comfort in war. Peace is an altogether more worrying prospect: not knowing such peace; not knowing what it might entail; how you decide winners and losers. These are the mind games that are part of the fight.

As the script of 1993 played out, there was a story of a video which contained that IRA ultimatum of talks or war. And then a page turn, to a statement given to me in a darkened room on a November afternoon on the Shankill Road, which painted a picture of that next crossroads at which loyalists had arrived. This was before the news emerged of the secret talks between the British and the IRA. We were running just to try to keep up with each development, at times not knowing which way to turn or who or what to believe. And, these many years later, we know that some of what we were seeing then was not as it seemed. For instance, there was a remarkable effort to bring that story of the British–IRA talks to public attention. Who benefitted from that revelation? Not the UK government, nor then Prime Minister John Major or Northern Ireland Secretary of State Sir Patrick Mayhew.

Before dealing in detail with those secret contacts, I want to rewind to April 1993. The video given to me by the IRA that month was its response to a peace mood that was getting louder. It was inside an envelope dropped onto a table where I was sitting alone in west Belfast. The man who left it said just a few words as he walked away. Something like, 'That's for you, Brian.' No introduction; no indication of what was in the package; no clues; no nothing. When I got back to the office there was a big decision to be made. The IRA had recorded its Easter message on the video: there were words read by a woman, music and pictures of the IRA with heavy weapons and test-firing a mortar bomb. The decision about whether or not to broadcast it was above my pay grade. One of the editors, Tom Kelly, was in the office. The then BBC controller in Belfast, Robin Walsh, would have been consulted.

The BBC decided to use it – not the voice of the woman reading the statement, but the pictures, with scripted lines from me on the message it contained. The introduction to one of my news reports on 9 April 1993 read as follows: 'The IRA has said Britain must choose between peace and what it calls the inevitability of war. The message is contained in a propaganda video released to the media by the IRA today. Its release comes twenty-four hours after Gordon Wilson said that his meeting with the IRA had not brought peace one inch nearer.' Wilson's young daughter, Marie, was one of those killed by the IRA in the Enniskillen Remembrance Day bomb in 1987. There was no reference in that introduction to my news report as to how that video had been given to me. And soon after the news that evening, I made myself unavailable for a few days and took an Easter break. I did not want to speak with the police – the RUC had contacted the office. Over the next couple of days, the newspaper headlines included: 'Storm rages after BBC screens IRA "war video"', 'Provo's chilling threat', 'IRA in video of hate', 'Provo tape issues a new "declaration of war"', 'IRA defies wave of peace with chilling video', 'IRA militants seen to be in ascendancy'.

Under its headline, 'IRA in video of hate', the *Daily Mirror* chose these words as a summary of developments:

- The IRA released their own video nasty yesterday to peddle their message of hate.
- The three-minute film showing killer gangs on a training exercise was sent to TV stations in Belfast.
- The Provos billed the propaganda operation as their Easter message.
- And it promised more death and destruction on both sides of the Irish Sea.
- The merciless message was the IRA's answer to peace rallies in Britain and Ireland telling them to quit their terror campaign.

This is an instance when you become the news. The video was not sent to the BBC. I have described how it was given to me. Two days later, the *Sunday Tribune* reported:

> The BBC yesterday defended its decision to show an extract from an IRA propaganda video on its evening news programmes on Friday night. ITN and RTÉ did not run extracts, although both reported on the fact that they had received the video and described what it showed. A spokesperson for the BBC said a short extract, showing IRA members 'in action and preparing weapons' had been shown, 'because it was in the public interest to demonstrate the video's political significance in terms of the IRA's future intentions'. He said the clip, lasting several seconds, 'was clearly labelled as a propaganda film'.

*The Observer* reported: 'While the IRA has a tradition of releasing messages to coincide with the anniversary of the Easter Rising in 1916, its "corporate video" is a new departure.' *The Irish News* quoted the Fine Gael TD Austin Currie, who accused the BBC of 'disgraceful and irresponsible' behaviour and said it 'had allowed itself to be a propaganda tool for the IRA.'

It is so easy to shout from the outside. There is nothing simple about news in conflict. For all the controversy and headlines, I believe the decision was the right one. At this time there was an emphasis on peace. Just weeks earlier, two young boys had been killed by IRA bombs in Warrington. The rallies that followed were an appeal to the IRA to stop. That was also the purpose of Gordon Wilson's meeting with the IRA. Yet the IRA had chosen this method, its video, this 'new departure', as its response – war pictures to deliver an ultimatum: talks or else. Of course it was news. And, when we look back now, it is also a reminder about what we see in conflict, what we know – but, more importantly, what we don't see and what we don't know. Out of vision, the UK government was in that secret back-channel contact with the IRA. The video message may well have been intended as a public statement to be heard by Major and Mayhew and others at that time; tailored for that specific audience, not propaganda, but part of those arm's-length contacts already exploring possibilities. We would soon learn that governments don't talk to 'terrorists', except when they do.

Then there was that other dialogue. Hume–Adams was

about to become public. The fallout from the IRA video became part of the routine of this place and its 'Troubles'. Angry words, headlines, news for a couple of days – until there was something else to get angry about. And, right on cue, there was. I was in Sligo – part of my being unavailable – when another story broke. Adams was spotted visiting Hume in Derry. It was an arranged spotting, I am told, something choreographed by republicans. They wanted that story out. There were two stories now within a couple of days of each other: one dressed in the images of war and then this other scene in Derry – a confirmation of dialogue, part of an exploration of other possibilities, a willingness to talk. At the time, our eyes were not clear enough to be able to see how those two stories might join up into something different. So, the immediate focus became the criticism and the condemnation of the meeting. Why would anyone talk to Adams? In this moment, the video became yesterday's news, old hat – or old balaclavas. There was something else to talk about, something more to worry about, something more to be added to those loyalist statements delivered with threats and accompanied by their codewords.

Within days of the video controversy and that story of the Adams visit to Hume in Derry, I wrote a note of a meeting – a conversation I had with two of the UDA's brigadier leadership: the former soldier, now holding high paramilitary rank, and that older leader who survived the purge at the top of this organisation. He often called me 'son', and when he phoned our home and was asked who's calling, would answer, 'Just a friend.' Part of my note is the age profile of the six leaders who formed the so-called 'inner council': one in his mid-fifties, one late forties, one late thirties, two early thirties and one late twenties. Young men calling the shots, literally. Their emerging story on the pages of that open book.

In this period of Ulster's war there was a fascination, or fixation, with what they called the pan-nationalist front. They were obsessed by this concept. It was part of every conversation, every contact, every statement. In loyalist attacks and actions throughout 1993, we were reminded of their words on New Year's Eve – that threat to intensify the campaign to 'a ferocity never imagined'. There was plenty to write about in the 'war commentary' of the various loyalist magazines: killings; attempted assassinations; one threat, then the next. Four men shot dead in Castlerock. And a calendar or chronology that showed the targeting of Sinn Féin. Grenade attacks at the homes of Gerard McGuigan, who died in 2021, Joe Austin and Gerry Adams. I was at each of those scenes and interviewed all three men. Gun and bomb attacks at an office in the New Lodge in north Belfast. A gun attack on the home of Sinn Féin councillor Annie Armstrong in Twinbrook. A man shot dead while working at the home of Alex Maskey. Sean Lavery, the son of Sinn Féin representative Bobby Lavery, shot dead at their home in north Belfast.

In this onslaught, no one and nowhere was out of bounds. This was the threatened intensification of the UFF campaign: words, then bullets and grenades as proof of what they said and what they meant. This was a year when every word and every thought was about Hume–Adams, the Dublin government, the IRA and, how in the loyalist mind, they came together in this pan-nationalist front. I have a note of a conversation, in which a UDA leader said, 'Hume is to the SDLP what Paisley is to the DUP. He is a dictator.' I have no doubt that they thought about killing Hume.

The 'northern command' of the UFF then issued what they called a 'pre-autumn statement'; the type of billing or label you might get on a statement from the chancellor. The UFF version was about war, not the economy – an opportunity to speak again on its 'policy in relation to the pan-nationalist front'. Then, in September 1993, there was another statement:

> Last night, five active service units of the Ulster Freedom Fighters planted five one-pound devices at five pan-nationalist targets. Direct responsibility for the UFF carrying out further attacks lies with John Hume, who is continuing to sup with the Devil while the Devil's disciples carry on with their sectarian genocide against the loyalist people and their towns. To issue joint statements and then say it is being done in the name of peace, isn't worth two balls of roasted snow to the loyalist people.

In this statement, they were taunting Hume with his own words, words he had used previously to dismiss criticism of his dialogue with Adams, saying he did not care 'two balls of roasted snow', that his talks were about ending violence and a search for peace.

There were other statements from the UFF, widening their target list and saying, again, that attacks on the nationalist community would intensify. Then, immediately after the IRA bomb on the Shankill Road, there was a warning delivered in another set of loyalist words: 'John Hume, Gerry Adams and the nationalist electorate will pay a heavy, heavy price for today's atrocity which was signed, sealed and delivered by the cutting edge of the pan-nationalist front.' 'The crucible' had become a firing range on which any and every Catholic was a target.

Behind the statements and the bullets, there was a fear of Hume–Adams: what it might lead to; how the UK government might respond to an IRA peace; what it would mean for Northern Ireland, for the Union. I knew the loyalist leadership, every one of their names. They were that open book that I described earlier. I met them all; had meetings in Rathcoole, in east Belfast, south Belfast and, many times, on the Shankill Road, including in the office that was the target of the IRA bomb in that attack in October 1993. Nine civilians dead in the rubble with one of the IRA bombers. Not another 'mistake', but the inevitable consequences of what the IRA did that day. I never knew what was going to happen next; would never have wanted to know. But in the routine of these things, there was an inevitability. No one needed a crystal ball.

In this period, my phone never stopped. There was little

time at home. And there was no time to think. We were lost in that blizzard of war – its relentless pace, when practically every day was a story of more death. One Saturday on the Shankill Road, the following Saturday in Greysteel, and everything that happened in between. Everyone remembers those bloody days – a war that felt like hell. Some will never be able to forget what happened. Police and soldiers ran from one scene to the next; there were big arrest operations, including lifting Adair, to try to interrupt what was happening; an atmosphere of fear. Something raw – something not experienced on this scale for quite some time. A sense of absolute hopelessness. Gunfire. Words. Hume broken – few, now, seeing any worth in his talks with Adams. The two governments, British and Irish, running a mile from that dialogue. Then there were two other major developments, as a continuation of this year of headlines that described the crisis of 1993. The first was the story of another attempt by loyalists to bring a major arms shipment into Northern Ireland.

When I read back into this period, I find notes and scripts, and I wonder from where some of the thinking and the lines emerged at that time. Whether it was just a desperate hope for a miracle that would change things, or if there really were, actually, some straws in the brutal winds of then. Within days of that mad week I have just described, there was a statement from the IRA – a response to some public comments from Senator Gordon Wilson and the Presbyterian minister Roy Magee, who had been speaking with loyalists, mainly within the UDA, and exploring ways that could end the violence. Magee would come to be known as the 'Reverend Ceasefire'. The IRA said those public comments 'suggest the possibility of another temporary halt to the murder campaign by the loyalist death squads. Any cessation of murderous attacks against nationalists would, of course, be welcomed.' I asked a loyalist leader, the man who often called me 'son', if there was any possibility of this happening: 'Christ, no. Christ, no,' was his response. 'The people I would know wouldn't be doing anything unless there was a total cessation from the IRA side. You wouldn't get anything unless that happens,' he said. The IRA had misread the signals – or Wilson and Magee had.

There was a lull in the violence. Not the announcement of any temporary ceasefire, but some stepping back. And some thinking out about what needed to happen next. For republicans, there was an emphasis still on the Hume–Adams dialogue. And a few lines from the Combined Loyalist Military Command: 'In accordance with the overwhelming desire of the majority of our population, we are earnestly seeking peace. However, in the eventuality of peace being bought at any price, we are preparing for war. A definitive Combined Loyalist Military Command policy document will be issued soon. And no further statements will be made or authorised, except from this source.' That reference to a peace 'at any price' was an expression of fear, that constant worry, about what a government would give for an end to IRA violence. And we would come to learn that the reference to 'preparing for war' – meaning more war and some further escalation – was in relation to what they thought would happen next. A huge arms shipment was on its way to Northern Ireland. Some of those in that Combined Command would have known the detail of this; what it would mean for the loyalist war. It didn't get that far – the shipment was intercepted on its way here.

I have a crumpled, half-A4 page from that day when the weapons were seized. A yellow Post-it stuck on the back reads: 'UVF arms statement. November 24th '93'. The typed text runs to fourteen lines. In it, the seizure of weapons at Teesport in England was described as a 'logistical set-back' that 'in no way diminishes our ability nor our determination to carry on the war against the IRA'. There was a reference to 'these dark days'. A look out any window in Belfast or elsewhere at that time would confirm that dark mood, the rawness of the wounds that stretched from Shankill to Greysteel still very much there – those physical and mental wounds. That afternoon, 24 November 1993, I met with a number of loyalist leaders. David Ervine was present. I didn't know him then and he didn't introduce himself. He met me downstairs and brought me to a room where two men were waiting. Again, no introductions. I had met one of them before and knew the other – the most senior figure in the UVF. The purpose of the meeting was to give me the statement. I was asked to remove it from an envelope sitting on the table. I cannot remember how long that meeting lasted or much about the conversation. I suppose the statement spoke for itself.

These latest developments were a confirmation of advanced preparation for some further escalation of war in circumstances in which loyalists might feel that they had been sold out in some secret deal between 'their' government and the IRA. Three hundred rifles had been seized, handguns, ammunition, grenades, detonators and two tonnes of high explosive. Not then, but later, one of those UVF figures I met on the Shankill Road that day told me: 'Teesport was about equalising the situation. Putting our own forces on a level playing field [with the IRA].'

At that moment, another story was about to break; another tremor in this bloody year of earthquakes – a story of secret contacts, the British government communicating with the IRA – and the next crisis on that calendar of 1993.

# FIVE

# Secret Talks

## *A Letter to Willie*

WHEN I THINK ABOUT IT now, it was one of the cheekiest moves in the conflict period. Revealing the most secretive of stories but in a way that means you get someone else to do it for you – that person so far away from you that they would never suspect you of the leak. Then, many years later, you whisper it out – miles away from actual time now and when you no longer care who knows. Reporting a conflict on its journey to peace takes time and patience. This is one such story: of a British document, the IRA, a third party, a politician and the headline. Then there was the earthquake in which the UK government in London and Belfast felt the tremors. Major and Mayhew were in a corner.

You always have to think about two scenes: the one onstage and what you are missing offstage. There is an example of this in 1993, in the screaming headlines that were the confirmation of those contacts between the British government and the republican leadership. Back then, DUP MP William McCrea (now Lord McCrea) had the document to prove it. There would be no more denials. But who gave him the proof? In whose interest was it that this most secret and confidential of contacts, that had been happening periodically since the 1970s, should now become public? It has been one of the mysteries and one of the puzzles in the politics of this place – one of those offstage happenings that demands our attention. Not everything is as it seems. You need to watch carefully. What follows is the story of how the IRA manoeuvred that detail and that document into the headlines. McCrea knew and knows nothing of this. It took me years to obtain absolute confirmation.

It would be another of those convoluted dramas. It was late 1993 – night-time. The streets were dark and wet. A colleague, the late Davy Morgan, dropped me at a car park in west Belfast and waited for me to return. I could be a while. I stepped into the meeting place. A man, who was sitting, nodded at me to join him. The last time we met he had been wearing a balaclava, in a house somewhere, waiting to brief me on the executions of Dignam, Starrs and Burns. Like the last time, he did not introduce himself by name. But I knew I was in the company of P. O'Neill. He seemed uneasy that my colleague was outside, so we left by another door in order not to be seen. Then we walked. This was not an on-the-record meeting. He would have information for me. Not tonight though. And there were no specifics about the what or when. But, when the time came, I would have to attribute it to the DUP. Now, it was my turn to feel decidedly uneasy. Perhaps, to borrow a word from an earlier chapter and another meeting with the IRA, 'discomfited'. I said, 'No.'

Immediately, the mood changed. It became as dark as the night. I was told that this meeting had not taken place. I should not discuss it. There was some reference to how people could end up in body bags. I took that to mean me. We parted. I returned to the car park and told Morgan to say nothing about where we had been. He was confused. And so was I. Indeed, in my case, I was more than confused. I was worried. That night, I contacted Eamonn Mallie and we met in a burger place not far from the BBC. I explained what had happened – the gist of the conversation, the now non-meeting; what had been said about unspecified information that would be made available to me, and this condition that I should attribute it to the DUP. I explained that I had said no. Part of the conversation with Mallie was me wanting to know, needing to know, if he had been approached. Had he any idea about what was going on? He could tell I was unnerved by what had happened.

There had been no contact with him. But, as this story developed over time, McCrea would give a document to Mallie – the proof of government contact with the republican leadership. Eamonn had been chasing this story, doing his homework, following leads and asking questions. There had been hints and suggestions, a scent of something happening. And he was following that trail – hearing it denied by the Northern Ireland Office (NIO), being told that what he was asking about belonged on the pages of some spy thriller. McCrea's confirmation to Mallie changed the script. The story was out, the government flapping. Secretary of State Sir Patrick Mayhew was flummoxed, caught out. He was now in the headlights, with answers that only raised more questions. His news conference on the Sunday the story broke was a drama in itself. In the book *Reporting the Troubles* I wrote about these events, adding: 'The full details, only confirmed to me in 2017 and 2018, are for another page and another time.' This is the time. These are the pages. To tell the story of that dark meeting with the IRA and the remarkable events that followed – having the information now to solve the mystery.

Back in 1993, in the reporting of this developing story, there was no suggestion of the IRA being involved in the leak. But for years I had a question in my head, a suspicion – indeed, something much more than that. It was a constant thinking back to that walk in the dark, that bizarre and unsettling conversation about information that would be made available to me and that I would then have to attribute to the DUP. Was this it? Could I be certain? At that time, the answer was no. I understand now that there are circumstances which mean you have to allow for time to pass, enough time for sources to be more candid. You have to understand that they are not going to disclose details that will do damage, especially to them. So you wait, on occasions such as this, for them to arrive at a moment when they think it is safe to speak. I waited twenty-five years for the answers, for the certainty I needed. There was a first confirmation in 2017 and then a second, in 2018. Two different sources – two people very much in a position to know, speaking quietly, not loudly, about these events, about that fascinating period in our history and its writing; making sense of one of its chapters, joining the dots.

To go back all those years and to understand the twists and turns of that time, you have to know how things worked in that link between the government and the republican leadership. We did not know in 1993. It was a story that evolved over time. MI5 was involved, along with senior representatives of the republican leadership, Martin McGuinness and Gerry Kelly, while three Derry men, the late Brendan Duddy, Denis Bradley and Noel Gallagher, were in the middle, as the links between the main players. It was in 1996, not long before the IRA ceasefire collapsed in the London Docklands bomb, that I first asked Duddy if he had been involved in the secret contacts. It was the first time we had met. He denied it then but confirmed it many years later. Duddy was the link to the Security Service, to the British.

The story of the contacts, what we came to know as the 'back channel', first broke not long after the IRA Shankill bomb and the UVF's attempt to smuggle that huge arms shipment into Northern Ireland. It emerged when Northern Ireland was breaking under the strain of the political and security crises of those times. You can imagine the mood when it did. Mayhew had nowhere to hide. At a news conference on Sunday, 28 November 1993, just hours after Mallie ran the story, the Secretary of State looked visibly shaken by the emerging news; by a story that was never meant to get out. Yet, here it was, and here he was in a packed room with so many questions waiting for answers.

These kinds of days are different news days, days when a government cannot just roll its eyes to dismiss a question. This question already had its answer. We now knew that Major's government had been in contact with the republican leadership. Mayhew was involved at arm's length. This was his time to explain himself, in circumstances when every word of explanation would bring another question. Those in the room with me had reported the conflict for years, many more years than I had; they included Mallie, David McKittrick, Fionnuala O'Connor and Ed Moloney. The government was not going to bluff and bluster its way out of this one. This was not one of those moments when it could just walk away.

It was in response to a question I asked that Mayhew linked Martin McGuinness to a message passed to the government in February 1993 – a message he said was from the IRA leadership, that the conflict was over and that republicans needed British advice to bring it to a close. This was a remarkable revelation. It felt like he was kicking up dust, hoping for something to hide behind. Mayhew needed a reason – justification – to explain why a government would be in contact with the IRA when people were still being slaughtered on the streets. What better reason than the

IRA seeking help to end its war? Years later, in 1999, John Major would publish the text of that communication in his autobiography – a message from the leadership of the IRA that had come through an intelligence link, from that back channel. But by 2007, Duddy, now speaking publicly about his central role in the contacts, told me: 'Martin McGuinness was psychologically not capable of asking for British advice to end the conflict, the IRA's war. That is not in Martin McGuinness's make-up or character.'

Now, we know much more about this back channel and how it worked. I had originally thought about it as some type of postbox, into which the British and the republican leadership sent their messages, the type of urgent post that would have a first-class stamp, and another stamp to make sure of a swift delivery. That was a part of it, but it had a much wider role and purpose. When he eventually came to talk about it, Duddy told me of his many meetings with the British in which he shared his thinking and his analysis; what he thought needed to happen. So, there was much more to this than the agreed and controlled words exchanged between McGuinness and the British. This is how it gets to the point where it all becomes confused and breaks down, which is what happened in 1993.

Go back a few years to those moments I referenced earlier in this book. Another Secretary of State, Peter Brooke, thinking out loud about how it was difficult to envisage a military defeat of the IRA. Think of the question that then asked of the republican leadership. Could the IRA defeat the British?

After a period when it was dormant, Brooke sanctioned the reopening of the back channel. An arm's-length, deniable means of contact, which began to explore possibilities. The fact that McGuinness and Kelly were involved tells you all you need to know – that republicans viewed this as a significant and serious initiative, within which the possibility of direct engagement was being considered. To facilitate this, the IRA agreed to an unannounced ceasefire. Duddy delivered the message to the British. Then things fell apart before any face-to-face negotiations. So near, and yet so far. The public fallout was the document that William McCrea sent by fax to Mallie, the Mayhew news conference that followed, including what he said about McGuinness, then a two-sided battle on the content and the correspondence. What was right? What was wrong? All of this played out at the time. I won't re-run that script here. The British had to correct parts of their record.

For obvious reasons, they had been denying the contacts. In sensitive, high-risk, processes of this kind, it was, I suppose, a permissible lie. This was 1993 – the year of those bombs in Warrington and the bomb on the Shankill Road. John Major's numbers in parliament were not good. He needed the unionists, and he had spoken about how it would turn his stomach to talk with republicans. This is one side of the coin. There was, of course, another side. Republicans needed talks if there was to be any chance of peace – talks with the enemy; talks with the 'Brits'. We couldn't read the tea leaves then. But, when I look back now, I see things very differently. More clearly. The fog of war out of my eyes. The

IRA video at Easter 1993 was as much about peace as it was about war. Manoeuvring the Hume–Adams talks into a space where they could be seen was proof of a willingness to engage in dialogue and to explore alternatives to arms. Then, the evidence of those British–republican contacts is a story that says, even in war all things are possible. Governments do talk with 'terrorists'. From a distance to begin with, and it is denied, of course, until it is no longer deniable.

How then did the IRA come to have the proof of the contacts? A document was delivered to Duddy to pass to McGuinness. There was a message to explain it – an introduction, or an explanation, I suppose, read from an aide-memoire by a member of MI5. Duddy would write that message down to repeat to McGuinness and, in normal circumstances, the official acting on behalf of the government would take the aide-memoire away. This time, he left it. Years later, a source would comment: 'Either by accident or design, republicans are handed a smoking gun.' Duddy gave it to McGuinness. Republicans now had a document to prove their contacts with the British. And, in late 1993, they decided to use it. The question was how to use it and how to achieve what they wanted in a way that would not be traced back to them. Part of what happened next was that walk in the dark with P. O'Neill explained earlier in this chapter; that conversation about unspecified information that he would share with me if I would attribute it to the DUP. I was not prepared to do that, though I would have been prepared to use the information without any attribution.

Unknown to me then, I was in some wider frame. Republicans had worked out a plan to get the document to McCrea in a way that would not be obvious. They were covering their tracks. McCrea knew nothing of this. Nor did Mallie when the document was eventually shared with him. Nor did anyone else in that chain of events. As the story is told to me, the document was meant to be handed to McCrea by someone whose identity I do not have – not a republican, but by someone who, unwittingly, was being used. The suggestion is he got cold feet, left the document with someone else and it was posted – to the wrong address – before arriving with McCrea. Once McCrea shared it with Mallie, it was only a matter of time before we would read it and hear it in the headlines – the back channel, those contacts, no longer a secret. It took me years to iron out the wrinkles in this story.

I have a note I wrote in my archive, me thinking around these events, that republicans wanted to get past the barrier the British had erected of no talks with Sinn Féin until there was a genuine end to violence. And that the back-channel contacts would prove that Britain had no principled objection to talking, even as that violence continued. It was in the IRA's interest to manage how the story got out. I wrote that note in April 2010, but I still had no confirmation that that was what happened in 1993. No one in the chain of events, including the third party, knew of the IRA's involvement.

I don't know how that third party was approached. I haven't been told. So, we can only guess. It was possibly by someone posing as a concerned official. We could speculate about the possible lines used. That they had learned of these contacts, were worried about what was happening and wanted the story out. Is that what happened? I don't know. Could it have happened that way? It is possible. The absolute confirmation that it was republicans who leaked the document was given to me in April 2018, almost twenty-five years after the story was shouted out in the headlines. The purpose of the leak, I was told, was to expose what republicans regarded as the hypocrisy of the publicly expressed British preconditions for Sinn Féin's entry into talks, when, already, the government was involved in these secret contacts.

In his autobiography, John Major writes: 'The source of the leak was never found.' If the British were looking in their own system, then they were looking in the wrong place. As I retraced my steps, one of the lines I read was that: 'Adams wanted the talks story out.' I have no doubt about that. About a fortnight before the news broke, there were two briefings conducted by a republican. They happened on 15–16 November 1993. On 15 November I was told that the contact between the British and the republican leadership was 'cleared at the highest level on both sides'. Then, on 16 November, that at the Sinn Féin end of the protracted dialogue, the key figure was Martin McGuinness. In at least one of those meetings, I was accompanied by Eamonn Mallie. Two days later, McGuinness said, 'I can confirm that I was involved in direct and protracted contact and dialogue with the British government. This contact was at an official level and no pre-conditions were set upon it.' But where was the proof? That was still some days away, in the form of that aide-memoire and the news coverage it generated.

Over many years, I have told this story using pieces of a jigsaw puzzle. This is the fullest picture I have. It's not all of the picture – there is always something missing, something more. There was so much going on in 1993 that was never meant to be seen. But we know now what it was: the beginnings of some effort to escape the mayhem of those times; the first contacts that were about trying to change things; two dialogues that were the start of that – Hume–Adams and the back channel. That the latter ended in the mess of 1993 is no surprise. It was behind the scenes. There were too many links in the chain, no trust, and too much information and analysis in the process coming from Duddy and the other link men trying to interpret McGuinness. And, in some cases, this was all being misinterpreted by the British as his words. The February 1993 message that Mayhew and Major reference is an example of this. It was an analysis from the back channel, to which Denis Bradley believes someone in the British system added the line about the conflict being over and needing British advice to bring it to a close.

The government version of the back channel is that it was a link to the IRA through MI5. Republicans disagree, saying it was a link to Sinn Féin. Yet, P. O'Neill was involved in the events of late 1993, including that walk in the dark with me.

He would not have been involved if this was not the business of the IRA. The learning in this episode was that a wider, more open dialogue was needed. Adams wanted those talks. The British needed an end to violence to move to a more open phase of negotiation.

The Downing Street Declaration of December 1993 was the governments of Ireland and Britain, and the two Prime Ministers, John Major and Albert Reynolds, trying to take back control of things. The Combined Loyalist Military Command restated its position in relation to IRA violence. Unless something changed in respect of that, there would be no change on the loyalist side. The Combined Command also called for a forum to be established to encompass loyalists and the unionist political parties. Gerry Adams said building a peace process would not be easy. It would be difficult, dangerous and protracted. And, as we waited for 1994, there were these other words: 'The UDA and UFF exist because the government has abdicated its responsibility to protect the Northern Ireland state and its citizens. So long as the pan-nationalist terror and political coercion continues, we retain the right to respond militarily in 1994.'

We understand now that trenches are dug deeper before people decide to come out of them. There were times in 1993 when peace seemed a million miles away. No closer. No hope. No chance. But, perhaps, this was the moment when everyone began to properly understand the consequences of failure. That week in October was a reminder of the worst years and the worst times in the conflict – the dead, the tears, the funerals – one after another. The hate in the air. The political noise. People in bits. Something had to change. And we know now that that required one of the sides to take a first step out into some unknown – an initiative and a risk for peace. At the time, we had no idea just how quickly things would move. We had no sense of opportunity, but we were at the window of a new day.

# SIX

# Ceasefires
*'We'll come to you'*

THE YEAR 1994 WOULD BE the same and, there again, different. The same actions and words from the IRA and the loyalist organisations, then different words that forced us to readjust our television sets and retune our radios. I would start to hear different conversations, new words that would be the beginning of some different news. At first, it was hard to comprehend. We were still seeing the 'war' thing, while, at the same time, hearing the beginnings of this 'peace' thing. The task then involved working out that contradiction, trying to see through the confusion, the conundrum that was, and can still be, this place. The people I had talked with for years were now talking about other things – quietly to begin with. It could be described as learning a second language, one that translated war into peace, into an 'unarmed strategy'. I remember the first time I heard it: where I was, and my sitting up and paying more attention. We were turning a word bend onto some new road. This was in the late summer, early autumn of 1994. There would be big moments of decision for the IRA and then the loyalist leadership. Questions about which road to take and how far to go for peace. There were times when they would get lost, but we were now outside the routine of the old story and the old ways. We would learn that some were more ready for the journey than others. It became a story of the doubters and the believers. This place was on a switch. There could be new words one day and the old ways another day.

I was asked in 2021 what the ceasefires meant to me, to set aside for a moment the politics of it all and to think and talk about how I felt personally. I spoke about the morning of 31 August 1994. It was Val's birthday and she was eight months pregnant. I had a meeting later that morning, at a time still to be fixed. I would be given the arrangements on my journey to work, delivered in a brief telephone conversation – no niceties, no names, just a message: 'Same place as Saturday, 11 o'clock. Bring Eamonn.' We were going to meet the IRA again, this time in very different circumstances. On this occasion, we would meet with a woman we both knew. I got a coffee and sat down beside her, in another of those places of tea and conversation. We were in the heart of a busy shopping complex in west Belfast.

It was another of those settings in which Mallie and I would stick out like sore thumbs – too obvious. You can imagine the scene, this moment in our times; the excitement; the energy. There was an electricity in the news that would light up new possibilities, perhaps herald new beginnings. We were like two cats on a hot tin roof – anticipating the words, not having the patience to hear them all but having to wait for the woman to read to the end. Her job done, she couldn't get out of the place quickly enough, get away from us quickly enough. Mallie and I couldn't get on to our phones quickly enough. There was a big line in that statement. Val would now share a birthday with the IRA's 'complete cessation of military operations', whatever that meant.

Earlier that morning, I had made my arrangements at the BBC. When I had the statement, I was to make a quick phone call to one of the editors, Tom Kelly. Donna Traynor would be in a radio studio ready to read the newsflash. Others would be in position to do the same on television. How did I feel? How did you feel? This was a day of mixed emotions for us all. It wasn't a day to get lost in the excitement of the words, but rather a moment to measure steps and to measure hope. Others were ahead of us – those in the IRA leadership, who had been thinking about the journey and working out the route, clearing a path for others to follow. They knew the way to this point and to that statement on 31 August 1994. We had some catching up to do.

Our starting point was that meeting and those words the woman read to us in the cafeteria in west Belfast that morning. I had been there before and knew the owner, Gerry Moynes. He lives in my home town and would have seen me in his place periodically over a number of years, would have known my work, but he never asked me about any of that. Recently, I bumped into him when he was having a Sunday drink in Holywood. I got his number and, the next day, asked him for a few words to take us back to those days in the 1990s: 'Once you came in, we knew that you weren't in to look at the menu,' he said, adding that it was obvious that 'there was going to be "a meet" of some description'. On 31 August 1994, the 'special' at 'The Patio' was a first – word ingredients of a different kind; something very new on our plates.

Out of our vision, the drafting of the IRA statement was completed in the period 28–29 August. Some small amendments that had been suggested by the then Taoiseach Albert Reynolds were made, while others were rejected. P. O'Neill travelled to Monaghan on 29 August and was in Dublin the following day. Before he left Belfast, the proposed IRA statement had been typed and recorded somewhere in the city, and arrangements for its distribution had been agreed pending a final decision on timing. There was still a possibility that it would be released on 30 August, but last-minute negotiations over a visa for veteran republican Joe Cahill to travel to the United States delayed its release until the following day. P. O'Neill was not directly involved in any of the meetings with journalists in Belfast or Dublin. Under his direction, others acted on his behalf.

Our daughter, Elle, was born on 22 September, in between the IRA and the loyalist ceasefire announcements of that year. Not long after Val brought her home from hospital, one of the UDA 'brigadiers' called me. He needed to see me. I explained what was happening at home. 'We'll come to you' was his response when asked if it was urgent. They did. I met them at the maypole in Holywood's High Street and took them to Claudia's coffee shop. One of them was looking for something 'substantial' to eat. Perhaps, the lasagne. It was far too early for that. I think I ordered three coffees and three scones. These were the beginnings of the out-of-war moments and the out-of-war meetings. Things were more relaxed now. There were no specifics on timing, but now that their concerns were being addressed, loyalists were moving towards their own ceasefire. They would be in touch.

The Church of Ireland Archbishop Robin Eames (now Lord Eames) had been to see Prime Minister John Major. The loyalist concern was about secret deals with the IRA. What price had been paid for this 'complete cessation of military operations'? What would be the cost to Ulster? At a news conference, Eames said the Prime Minister had given him his word that there had been 'no secret agreement' with the IRA. The churchman said he had been asked to make this information public. And he spoke directly to loyalists: 'There is more to be gained in the political sense through dialogue than will ever be gained through the barrel of a gun.' Eames' words had registered. It is why, a couple of weeks later, those loyalists had come to see me in Holywood.

How did I feel in those changing days of 1994? Unsure, I suppose. Uncertain. This was a new place. One step at a time. All of us were out of our routine. It might seem a strange thing to say or write, but we were out of the comfort zone of war. There were new lines in new scripts. Coffee in west Belfast.

Coffee at Claudia's. Strangers in my hometown. More people were out in the open. Were we really escaping the gunfire and that hell of the previous year? Would it happen so soon? We know now, of course, that this was the beginning of a long end.

On 12 October 1994, on the eve of the loyalist ceasefire announcement, I would see one of the men who came to meet me in Holywood. This time we were in a different place, with different company, at Woodvale at the top of the Shankill – that road in Belfast that knew the war; that, not even a year previously, was at the centre of the story of the bomb of 1993 and the statement on the big arms shipment that was caught before it got here. Now, on this night in 1994, there were three loyalists in the room: Joe English, John Graham and Winston Churchill Rea. They were there to set the scene for the next day. Their presence, together, was a statement in itself – a representation of loyalism in its broadest form; a leadership getting ready to speak its response to the IRA.

I was with Ivan Little of Ulster Television. There were other loyalists in the building. And in the many newsrooms, in Belfast and elsewhere, there was a building expectation that an announcement was close. It was even closer now. As this meeting ended, I would give the BBC a few lines for a newsflash. An 'unprecedented' news conference was scheduled for nine o'clock the next morning. It would involve the two loyalist parties, the Progressive Unionist Party (PUP) and the Ulster Democratic Party (UDP), and it would happen at Fernhill House on the Old Glencairn Road in west Belfast. Gusty Spence gave Little and I those few lines typed on a page. He had timed and dated this statement: Belfast 9.55 p.m., Wednesday 12 October 1994. That detail was all part of arranging the stage, all part of a building excitement. The ceasefire was now imminent. We would hear it described more fully in about eleven hours' time. And those emerging faces in that community would occupy the top table – Davy Adams, David Ervine, Gary McMichael, William 'Plum' Smith chairing, Gusty Spence, John White and Jim McDonald. All but White wore shirts and ties. Spence drew on his pipe. The headline was that, from midnight, the Combined Loyalist Military Command 'will universally cease all operational hostilities'. Here was another moment in our changing story.

I have kept all of my notes – the statements, some of the speeches, the magazines and the newspapers, this evidence of the chronology and the creativity of it all; how the words made different sounds, meant different things. It was all part of the making of these better times. And to go back to that question: how did I feel, personally? These were moments in history, better understood now, better appreciated now than then. To be there, to hear those new words, to watch these developments across the different sides and lines, was to have a front-row seat. In a sporting context, many would have paid big money for my ticket. I live here. I lived with that war – had a young family now, including a baby girl just a few weeks old. There was a chance now. Possibilities. But mistakes were made. The British government and the unionist political leadership were too slow to react, not trusting the enemy; not knowing what to do, so doing nothing other than repeating the same demands about decontamination and decommissioning. The IRA ceasefire was too much for them. In a sense, it was too good. The worlds of security and intelligence had not expected this 'complete cessation of military operations', but rather a ceasefire that would be time-limited and more conditional. Something that could have been more easily dismissed as not being good enough. So they were thrown by the quality of the statement. This is what I mean about it being too good. There was no plan other than to stall.

Think about it now – the madness of that. Surely you don't slow down peace; you get on with it. But they didn't, and it broke. They were asking for something akin to surrender. For all their intelligence, they didn't understand the stupidity and the foolishness of that. So, on 9 February 1996, an IRA bomb exploded in London Docklands. The hopes of that early peace were now part of the rubble of that day – two dead and war back in the headlines. Televisions and radios returned to their old settings. Was there a straw that broke the ceasefire's back? It's a question I asked of a senior police officer in 1997: 'I don't think there is such a straw,' he replied. ' I think it was a growing strain, if you like.' That growing strain was a reference to political dithering and delay. I think republicans and loyalists and those in the high ranks of policing here at that time, especially Ronnie Flanagan, better understood the ceasefires and this moment of opportunity than those in government and politics. They knew the pulse of war; that a possible treatment had been found and that we were in a moment that had to be nurtured. There was no time and no place for indecision.

As the process developed, I remember some of the things that Flanagan talked about. That you could not decommission the IRA's engineering knowledge, its ability to produce improvised mortar bombs and rockets and other devices. So, the emphasis should be on decommissioning the war mindset. He spoke also of the importance of avoiding splits and ruptures within these organisations; the challenge of cohesiveness; leaderships holding on to the critical mass. In his thinking, he was miles ahead of the politics. He was exploring the dictionaries and the maps and the means of peace. He called out unclaimed loyalist and IRA actions. And, in a way that no one else could have, years later, he delivered the RUC into a period of painful reforms, during which its name was changed. Flanagan was a leader in the peace, something that is not often acknowledged. McGuinness and Adams were leaders. So too was John Hume, and those loyalists I met on the Woodvale Road on the eve of their ceasefire announcement, among them Gusty Spence, who was there at the beginning of conflict and, now, in this new place – at the long beginning towards some end. They gave those first moments of peace over to politics, and found some more willing than others to explore their possibilities.

I spoke with Flanagan on the phone on 18 July 1997. Days earlier, we had had words about my criticism of the policing operation during that year's Drumcree marching stand-off and Flanagan's decision to clear the road for the Orange parade to go through; the last time it did. He was angry. He believed that, in my news and analysis, I had failed to give proper consideration to the calculations that he had to make, how he had to consider the different threats, try to balance the impossible weights of those decisions. It was not the first time that we had words, nor would it be the last time. There has to be space in these working relationships to disagree, to try to understand each other and the different roles we have, the different responsibilities. Peace adds to those responsibilities. It asks us to take more careful steps, to give more consideration to our words – particularly in a place so small.

When I called him on 18 July, I had just travelled the short distance from Moville in Donegal to the BBC Radio Foyle studios in Derry. My oldest son, Ruairi, who was ten, was with me. I had left Val in Moville with Elle and our new baby, PJ, who was just two months old. We were a couple of hours into a family break, and passing through the Redcastle Hotel, when work called. It was one of the news editors, Noel McCartney. There had been a statement from Sinn Féin. Adams and McGuinness had provided 'a detailed report and assessment to the IRA' and had urged the leadership to restore the cessation of August 1994. I told him that meant it was going to happen. He had a jacket, shirt and tie waiting for me in Derry. I told Val I would be as quick as I could.

My diary has details of television interviews at 6.30 p.m. and on a news special at 9.28 p.m., plus news reports on Radio Ulster that evening and early the next morning. When I called Flanagan, I could not be sure of his reaction. I was thinking about those words we had exchanged some days earlier, that disagreement. I need not have worried. He gave me a clear assessment. Recently, I reread one of my scribbled notes that I used in the interviews on that July evening. 'Security sources confident that a ceasefire is coming.' Their view was that 'Gerry Adams wouldn't make a statement of this nature if he wasn't confident of his position, if he wasn't confident of a positive outcome', and that those with whom I had spoken believed a ceasefire announcement 'could be imminent'. I believe I also spoke with a senior security official at the NIO. Then, I was called by a republican who advised me to get back to Belfast. Before leaving Radio Foyle on 18 July, I recorded a news report to play out the next morning and, first thing on the 19th, started the journey to the BBC, leaving Val in Moville with the kids. I would get back that night.

This is that early morning news script from 19 July 1997:

> Security sources are confident that a new ceasefire is coming and have been saying since yesterday evening that an announcement is imminent. Imminent is also the word used by a republican source, although he declined to be any more specific. The Gerry Adams statement of yesterday is being viewed as a clear signal, pointing the way to a new cessation. He and

Martin McGuinness have given the IRA an assessment of the situation and have urged the leadership of that organisation to renew its ceasefire. The two were the key players in the internal republican debate leading to the IRA ceasefire of August 1994 and both are hugely influential within the republican movement. Security sources say the IRA leadership has solid support within its ranks for a ceasefire and say there's nothing to suggest any division. The IRA has been active in recent weeks and, in the period following on from the Drumcree parade, looked to be stepping up its violent campaign. Now, things have swung in the opposite direction. Republicans believe a political package is in place to persuade the IRA to move and a new ceasefire now looks certain.

As that report was running, the republican I had spoken with the night before, Jim Gibney, called me to say the ceasefire statement had just been issued to RTÉ. It was an 'unequivocal restoration' of the 1994 cessation to take effect from midday on Sunday, 20 July 1997.

By now there was a new British government. Tony Blair had won a landslide victory just two months earlier. Mo Mowlam was NI Secretary of State. Sinn Féin had a key to talks. My television report on 19 July included some pictures of Flanagan at RUC headquarters, which I had arranged. We also had pictures of soldiers and police officers on the streets. These are some of the words I scripted for television:

Security forces on patrol in Belfast this afternoon. They've been advised to remain vigilant until the ceasefire comes into play. The Chief Constable, Ronnie Flanagan, at RUC headquarters this afternoon keeping an eye on developments. There's no specific intelligence that the IRA may be planning further attacks. The warning to security force members is a precautionary measure.

After the news that evening, I travelled back to Moville. I called the house where we were staying to say I was on my way and was told to hurry along. On that Friday and Saturday, I was away from the family for much longer than I anticipated – not for the first time. On many occasions since, that Redcastle, Moville, Greencastle neck of the woods has been our escape. It's not far, but a place well away from the wars of the North. At home, we are still suffocated by a past that talks to us, reminding us of its presence; every day is an anniversary.

The new ceasefire meant the peace process now had a second chance. But the old arguments lingered. The IRA still had its guns. So did every other side but, in all of the commentary, that seemed less important, not as pressing. The next and new reporting phase would take us to that point where 'peace' meets politics, and what needed to happen to make it work. Building trust is a long process. For a period of some decades, the different sides only had to condemn each other. Now, they had to think about talking with each other, working with each other – finding the ways and words that might eventually lead to some trust. These were the battles of the late 1990s. Things moved slowly to begin with; at times, they are still slow – peace is not easy.

Blair, Mowlam and Taoiseach Bertie Ahern had international help. There would be talks with purpose. This time, all of the right people were in the rooms, including republicans and loyalists, leading to the historic agreement on Good Friday 1998. It was a political rising, if you like, five years after that hell of 1993. Anyone who thinks that agreement was easy for any side needs to think again. There is no such road out of war. For everyone in that process, there were compromises to be made, difficult bends to negotiate, reassurance to be given, doubt wrestling with hope. In my documenting of the transition from conflict into peace, I would periodically record long interviews with a range of key figures. I did so when events were fresh in their minds, just to have their thoughts and memory for times such as this, so I could listen back and hear people, such as Flanagan and Adams, reflect on key moments. At times, when I reach into that archive, I am listening to the dead, a reminder of those who have left us, including David Ervine.

For this part of the book, I listened to two cassettes on an old machine borrowed for this purpose. The interviews were recorded on 25 May 1998 and 23 February 1999. I was talking to Ervine about those last days and hours leading to the Belfast/Good Friday Agreement. There was a nervousness as a late text was produced inside the talks and as decision time approached. This is a transcript of some of what he had to say. It is history on tape:

> First of all, I have to make it clear that Billy Hutchinson, myself and Hugh Smyth were quite frankly not prepared to take upon our shoulders alone the responsibility of continuing onwards, if you like, and therefore we had to broaden the levels of responsibility required. And whilst the PUP were doing the negotiating, it was fairly clear and I'm not likely to pull the wool over your eyes, or anybody else's for that matter, by telling you that the UVF weren't involved. They were heavily involved and we made sure they were heavily involved.

A late draft for consideration had caused concern. Ervine spoke of feeling 'pinned to the wall, because in some ways they were looking at us and saying, how to hell did you get us into this position?' According to Ervine, the days through to Good Friday were then spent negotiating away from that draft:

> At one point, in the last couple of days of negotiations at Castle Buildings, we had fifty-seven people in the room, in one of the larger conference rooms that we commandeered. And, then when the final draft came out, early on the Friday morning, we went through it line by line ... the leadership of the UVF and beyond were there, because, I think, they were conscious that

they wanted as many people involved as possible. Not from the point of view of having a crutch, but, genuinely, a point of view of assessing how well this is a sellable commodity. And they did that, and there were people from all over the country there. And, of course, in the middle of the night, we dispatched people to Long Kesh, where they had a relatively swift meeting, but, nevertheless, an incisive meeting with the leadership of the UVF prisoners.

Ervine believed that Adams and McGuinness had navigated 'a treacherous and difficult journey' in making the agreement – an agreement we all know was below the bar of republican demands and expectations. 'Quite amazing,' he said. This is Ervine speaking in May 1998: 'And I don't think we could have anything other than a degree of respect about that. That doesn't necessarily mean that we respect them as people. We don't know them as people. Maybe that will come at a later date.' In 2007 Adams attended Ervine's funeral – a remarkable moment in the peace; a visual expression of how these two people had come to know and respect each other.

Beyond that political agreement in 1998, we were in a better place. Not yet a safe place, but safer. Before and after the agreement, Adams and McGuinness were fighting internal battles. They kept that critical mass that Flanagan referenced, but they lost people to a range of dissident IRA groups. Those same people periodically merged and emerged under new titles and in different balaclavas. It is out of these developments that the Omagh bomb of 1998 happened. The dead on that day are a reminder, if needed, of the fragility and the uncertainty of peace.

The phase of the process stretching from 1997 through to 2006 would bring me into contact with three more men in the role of P. O'Neill: 'Peter', 'Conor' and 'Tomás' – not their real names, of course. Their many statements represented the mainstream IRA tiptoeing on the eggshell of peace, trying not to break it, trying to hold their organisation together, measuring everything and every step and every word – those thousands of words that would be read to me and handed to me in this phase of the process. Adams and McGuinness were fighting those leadership battles inside, and political battles outside. Peace was proving a harder thing to control and to manage – not as 'easy' as the war. There would be statements on 'the disappeared', 'silent' guns, decommissioning and the ending of the armed campaign. And they were all, incrementally, delivered and balanced against other changes.

We would learn that peace doesn't come in a box with building instructions. Over the years, I have said many times that peace happens and doesn't happen. I would have my own battles with the P. O'Neills of this period. At times, communication would end. There were battles not just with P. O'Neill, but with others involved in this making of our new roads. People were much more sensitive in peace. Negotiations, involving compromise, are never easy. There were different pressures now – phone calls from all sides at

What seems like a lifetime ago, with Pat Grant in the BBC newsroom –
a period when the story was the 'Hell' of our times.

**Irish News**

AND BELFAST MORNING NEWS

THURSDAY, JULY 6, 1989

July 1989, with Val on the front page. One of those summertime snaps of
people enjoying the sun and their lunch in the grounds of Belfast City Hall.

Walking into one of those frames that was life in west Belfast during the conflict years. A major police operation. The media on the scene. The madness and 'normality' of it all captured within this frame.

1992, reporting from Crumlin Road Gaol in north Belfast, months after an IRA bomb behind bars had killed two loyalist prisoners. (Courtesy of Marty Johnston)

General Sir John Wilsey in a BBC interview with me in January 1993, where he stepped onto a banana skin, saying the army was 'certainly not ashamed' after its agent Brian Nelson was jailed. (Courtesy of Marty Johnston)

August 1994, the IRA ceasefire – one of those days when you run with the news and don't get tired.

January 1998, just days after the murder of Billy Wright inside the jail, the media was given rare access to the wings of the Maze Prison. It was a chance to speak with the loyalist and IRA leaderships – with Johnny Adair (top) on one wing and Padraic Wilson (bottom, far right) on another.
(Courtesy of BBC Newsline)

## GAE LARIN
## (Go Learn)Project
Tele/Fax:- 01232 – 469674

# Fax

| To: Brian Rowan | From: East Belfast Prisoners Aid P.C.R.G |
|---|---|
| Fax: 469674 | Date: 15·5·98 |
| Phone: | Pages: 1 |
| Re: | CC: Pat Longstein |

☑ Urgent   ☐ For Review   ☐ Please Comment   ☐ Please Reply   ☐ Please Recycle

**•Comments:**

Dear Brian,
I am writing to confirm
that it is Michael Stones wish not to
have his interview Broadcast due to
the sensitive nature and the Political
climate at the moment. It is not
our wish to cause any undue
stress or hurt in our community.

Michael Stone

In the Community
interest

Gae Larin (Ulster-Scotts,Go learn) - Equal Community Project

Frankie Gallagher
Development officer

May 1998, to me – a fax from the loyalist killer Michael Stone.

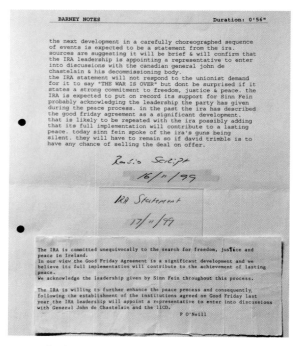

The choreographed steps of negotiations and peace-building. November 1999, a unionist source gave me the words the IRA would speak the next day. It was perfect guidance and a news exclusive on what would follow in a statement from P. O'Neill.

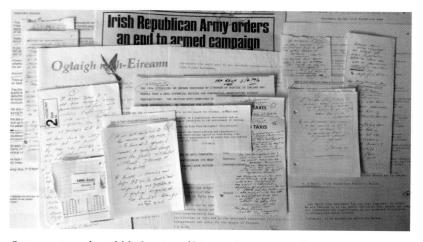

Statements and scribbled notes of history from some of my many meetings with the P. O'Neills.

Breaking news in a borrowed jacket and tie – discussing the latest twist in
the 'Stakeknife' story with Noel Thompson. (Courtesy of BBC Newsline)

Face to balaclava – long into the peace, an interview with the UVF.
(Courtesy of John Nicholson)

On a dander on Holywood High Street with the former chief constable
Sir Ronnie Flanagan. He was one of the leaders in the peace.
(Courtesy of M.T. Hurson)

December 2006. A sketch that tells a story of a few pints with David Ervine and my lost phone. How did it get into that bush? (Courtesy of R. Mills)

Peace is an endless political negotiation. In studio with Mark Carruthers and Eamonn Mallie discussing the Stormont 'Purgatory'.

In the middle of things. Adams arrested and me listening to McGuinness at a republican protest in Belfast. (Courtesy of @Bronac7)

I was going to the shop for a pint of milk – don't know what he was doing. With long-time colleague and friend Mervyn Jess at one of those policing scenes in the peace. (Courtesy of Albert Kirk)

The past still with us. Many voices heard in this event behind closed doors.
Our story still a war of lies and that 'Holy Grail' of truth.
(Courtesy of Healing Through Remembering)

Acclaimed artist Colin Davidson trying not to laugh. I must have been
telling him about my paint by numbers. (Courtesy of Colm McGlone)

July 2022, scribbling a few thoughts before speaking at the Glencree Peace Centre on the legacy of violence. (Courtesy of Colm McGlone)

With Val – chauffeur, confidante and the calm voice that talked me through the worst of times.

different times unnerved by what I said, or what they thought
I said, on radio or television. We were learning that peace is
a nervous thing, not sure of itself, not confident, not always
in the front row with its hand up. It's often shy and sitting at
the back.

The big battle immediately after the Belfast/Good Friday
Agreement was how to implement it. How to manage it
beyond that day of history. These were the hysterics in peace.
What were the medications and the counselling that would
be needed to keep it well as these new conditions emerged?
How to manage prisoner releases and police reform; the
problems in politics when the question of guns is not yet
answered; people wanting to control the news. What is good
for peace? What is bad for peace?

Between the agreement and the referendum, when people would have their say, I met with Michael Stone for the
purpose of a television interview with the BBC. He was on
parole. This was the man of guns and grenades and murder in Milltown Cemetery in 1988, and, these ten years
later, it would be a day of drama – in front of the camera
and behind the scenes. Days later, there was a Sunday headline: 'Row rages over killer Stone's TV interview'. It was a
newspaper exclusive. The opening paragraphs read: 'The
BBC, the Prime Minister and the UDP were embroiled in a
fierce behind the scenes confrontation over the broadcasting
of an interview with loyalist killer Michael Stone. For Tony
Blair is understood to have become personally involved in
attempts to stop the interview taking place, and when that

failed, being broadcast.' The newspaper did not speak with me. It had details of a fax from Stone, which was sent to the BBC newsroom – a move to try to stop the item from getting to air.

This is what happened that day and then later. The interview was on Friday, 15 May 1998. The previous evening Stone was paraded at a loyalist rally in the Ulster Hall in Belfast. This, just days after members of the 'Balcombe Street Gang', who had been serving long jail sentences in England, had appeared at the Sinn Féin Ard-Fheis in Dublin. This issue of prisoners, and the proposed early releases, was now large in people's minds, and this was before they had voted on the agreement. The governments were nervous – understandably so. By arrangement, I met Stone in east Belfast. One of the UDA 'brigadiers', Jim Gray, was there, as was John White, who had one of those seats at the loyalist top table when their ceasefire was announced in 1994. When the interview ended, I went outside to wait for Stone, to film with him in the street. I remember a phone ringing as I stepped outside. It was White's phone. I waited with the cameraman, but Stone didn't join us.

I went back inside, into a small room. White and Stone were seated, and Gray was standing at the door. I knew immediately that there was a problem. White asked me what I would say if they asked me for the tape. I said, 'No.' Then, what if Michael asked me for the tape? Again, I said, 'No.' I told them I was going back to the BBC and they could contact me there. By the time I got back, the UDP leader Gary

McMichael had been in contact with the newsroom. The fax was there. It was addressed to me and copied to the BBC controller Pat Loughrey, an indication of concern. It was written and signed by a loyalist, Frankie Gallagher, and also by Stone. It read: 'Dear Brian, I am writing to confirm that it is Michael Stone's wish not to have his interview broadcast due to the sensitive nature and the political climate at the moment. It is not our wish to cause any undue stress or hurt in our community.' The words, 'in the community interest', followed. Then, the signatures of Gallagher and Stone. But the prisoner issue was a significant part of the post-Agreement conversation, so it was important to hear what Stone had to say. The BBC ran the interview that evening.

Stone was the second UDA prisoner I had interviewed in the space of twenty-four hours. The previous day, I had been contacted from the jail by Sam McCrory and recorded an interview with him for radio. It was an attempt at damage limitation before Stone appeared at that Ulster Hall rally. McCrory, a Shankill loyalist and associate of Johnny Adair, was speaking on a mobile phone. He said the war was over and he apologised to the victims of violence. The next day, I asked Stone was that an apology he would want to share in:

> Stone: I would share in that most definitely. I have said in the past that all deaths are regrettable, be they innocent civilians, members of the security forces, loyalist volunteers and, yes, even members of the republican death squads.

Rowan: Do you apologise for what you did?

Stone: [pause] Within the context of being a volunteer in a war, no, I don't apologise, but I acknowledge the hurt I've caused.

With the referendum still to happen, it was not the type of answer the government wanted to hear – not on television, not on radio, not with people watching and listening, not from Stone, whose actions in the cemetery were filmed and on a rewind button inside many people's heads.

The issue of prisoner releases was poisonous. And more damage was being done. I was being blamed for some of that. Some time later, I cannot remember precisely when, Val and I were driving from Belfast along the Sydenham Bypass towards our home in Holywood. At traffic lights, she told me someone was trying to get my attention. When I looked, I saw this mop of blond hair. It was Jim Gray, leaning out of the window of the car beside us, guldering at me: 'Are you still stealing the fucking tapes? Are you still stealing the fucking tapes?' I looked at him in confusion and then I worked it out.

This was about the Stone interview. I was back in that small room in east Belfast. The tape I refused to give them in that moment, and then the panic when the political shit started hitting the fan. This was the fallout from the interview that the BBC had decided to broadcast against the wishes of loyalists and others, including those in government. I told

Val that if the car was still following us when we turned off at Palace Barracks into Holywood, to drive into the High Street and stop at the police station. It didn't follow us but continued on the road to Bangor.

People see the interviews, the bits on television, but not what happens behind the scenes – the dilemmas, the anger; at times, confrontations. Some years later, Gray was shot dead by his own people – a victim of one of the many internal loyalist wars. White had to run from Belfast as a result of another of those feuds. Alongside Johnny Adair, he was one of the most destabilising influences within that community. Why he had a seat at that ceasefire top table in 1994, I will never know. Years later, I wrote these words about Stone: 'In his war Michael Stone broke many people and many families, but his part in that conflict looks to have broken him also. That is not to excuse anything he did, not to offer sympathy. It is just an observation.'

Another interview I will never forget was with a loyalist who spoke to me about how prisoners sleep with their victims – meaning, of course, not being able to sleep or, in his case, make peace with what he did. Billy Giles was a life-sentence prisoner. He had completed that sentence when I interviewed him and, months later, hanged himself, unable to live with what he did. His is not a story that is told in headlines, but it should be – that in those seconds when he pulled a trigger and killed a young man, he also killed himself. It was a slow death with too much time to think. He had no answers to his own questions, no peace, no escape, no way out of his own guilt. He had years in jail, but his prison was inside his head: his actions, the replays; not something that ends in seconds, but lasts forever. A victim of the conflict? Who decides? I have spoken about this interview a number of times, including at an event one evening when someone suggested to me afterwards that I also 'sleep with the victims'. It was meant differently, of course. How I recall events. Remember them. The detail. The words. How small a place this is. How close the war was. What we brought home with us. How we can't let go. There are those who say it didn't affect them. I don't know how they created that physical and psychological distance. This place lives in what happened, lives with its dead and has not yet found peace of mind.

Post-agreement, after the referendum, the big wordplay and delay was on the issue of guns – those weapons that did so much damage, physical and mental. Guns that were quieter now, but still loud in this stand-off on decommissioning. The Ulster Unionist leader, David Trimble (who died in July 2022), refused to form a government until this question was addressed and answered. We would read all sorts of word contortions, hear the spin, and we would have to work our way through that muddle and that maze, trying to separate fact from fiction. My former BBC colleague Mark Simpson came up with the phrase 'more context than Semtex'. He allowed me to borrow it. I was told Adams wasn't amused. The three P. O'Neills I referenced earlier would speak on this issue from 1998 through to 2005 – exhausting the dictionary, exhausting Trimble's patience until he snapped.

The first 'act' of decommissioning was by one of the splinter loyalist factions, the Loyalist Volunteer Force (LVF). A small number of weapons was brought to the headquarters of the Independent International Commission on Decommissioning (IICD). It was December 1998, a week before Christmas. I was there, watching the sparks as the weapons were placed into grinders and fell into pieces. This was a play for the high ground; a play of words to go with the pictures; not real. Then, months later, on 28 May 1999, there were more words from this organisation that was supposedly on ceasefire. This time, they were about me. In news reports the previous evening, I had linked members of the LVF to the killing of solicitor Rosemary Nelson. They had placed a bomb under her car. This calendar of events will help explain the chronology:

- 15 May 1998, the LVF announced a ceasefire.
- 12 November 1998, the government recognised that ceasefire.
- 18 December 1998, first act of decommissioning by LVF.
- 15 March 1999, Rosemary Nelson killed by a bomb placed under her car.

The killing was claimed under the bogus organisational title of Red Hand Defenders. From mid-April 1999, I was hearing the names of those who placed the bomb, hearing this information from security sources. Then there was a conversation about the bomb-maker. Within loyalism, there was a short list of those with the ability to produce that device. By 18 May I had been told the identity of the bomb-maker – a 'freelancer' in this trade. The target had been chosen by Mark 'Swinger' Fulton, an LVF leader and once a close associate of Billy Wright. Both are now dead. On 27 May 1999, in news reports and radio analysis, I put the LVF in the frame, adding that I would not be surprised if they denied it. They did much more than that. In a meeting with journalists, they issued a statement of about forty lines – angry words, much of it directed at me and the BBC.

Commenting on my news reports, they said I had made a 'scurrilous statement'. Their ceasefire remained 'unequivocal and complete'. They had made a gesture of 'physical decommissioning of weapons'. It was 'ludicrous' to think 'we would be, at the same time, involved in carrying out military actions of the nature of the Nelson case'. The statement continued: 'We maintain the view that, only a political imbecile or one intent on causing new levels of mayhem in the country would put forth the statement that Brian Rowan and the BBC have made yesterday. We therefore call upon both parties to retract the statement or name the source of their so-called intelligence.' The final line read: 'Any actions deemed necessary by true loyalists shall be well thought through and decisive.'

There was no retraction. The statement was nonsense. The LVF was protesting too much. I believe I know the author of their words – one of the clowns of peace with an ego, who treated it all as a pantomime and a play. The assessment I had was correct. The information was confirmed years later at an inquiry.

While I described the LVF statement as nonsense, it was also worrying. I spoke with my Head of News, Andrew Colman, and contacted the Chief Constable, Ronnie Flanagan. Flanagan told me there was no information about any threat, but, if anything emerged, he would contact me immediately. That evening, at home, I had to tell Val about the statement. She had friends coming. They stayed the night. I remember them sitting across one of our front windows, when Val explained the statement to them. In the way of these things, there was a joke about them being human shields. It was one of those times when our humour saved us, kept us sane. The peace was not this pure thing that meant we were all safe. There would be moments like this – times that reminded us of the old ways. Times when I had to be more vigilant. Times when I worried about my safety and the safety of those around me.

Months later, there was another attempt to solve the guns and government conundrum that stood in the way of the politics of the Belfast/Good Friday Agreement and blocked the way to the formation of the power-sharing Executive. Senator George Mitchell was back, trying to take his work from the 1998 agreement through to its next stage, to implementation. It was called the Mitchell Review, a negotiation that arrived at a choreographed sequence of statements and developments. They were the logical next steps in a process that sometimes overemphasised, or overstated, or overrated, logic. In not buying into that logic, my neck was out like a giraffe. The big plan was that Trimble would take the first step – go into government with Sinn Féin – before there would be a start to decommissioning. But the logic of these things, in the thinking of some, was that an IRA move on arms would quickly follow, that it was inevitable. It all made sense. Except it didn't. I was hearing nothing about an imminent move on decommissioning, hearing that from a range of sources. I said it in my news coverage and pissed off those who thought differently. Had I been wrong, I would have walked away.

This was a big moment – not just for me, but for the BBC. The critical period was mid-November 1999. There was this choreographed sequence being shaped and almost ready to go. Three people were especially important to me in this moment: Martin McGuinness, the Unionist MP Ken Maginnis and Andrew Colman, the most senior BBC news editor in Belfast. More than anyone else in this period, I needed Colman's support. The context of a deal was changing from no guns–no government to no government– no guns. The emphasis now was on Trimble having to move first. Actual decommissioning was not an imminent prospect, but the IRA would appoint a representative to 'enter into discussions' with the IICD. On 9 November 1999 I was told of a set of words in the negotiation, what might become an IRA statement. That set of words had not yet been finalised and was still being worked on – part of the drafting and redrafting in negotiations of this kind. The source I was speaking with told me that if a whisper of this got out it could cause a reaction: 'Not that there would be any embarrassment to the most rabid activist,' he added. The words, this potential statement, were about 'testing the ground' inside the talks.

I intended to use the information that day, and did so. I spoke with a republican before I did, someone close to Adams. He wasn't amused. This is what he said: 'Entirely a matter for yourself. I know you are not messing, but whoever gave the information is messing. You have to make a judgement, not just about accurate or inaccurate, but is it helpful or unhelpful. I'm not confirming or denying.' His tone, his mood, was all the confirmation I needed. We had known each other a long time. If it was crap, he would have told me. I stepped into a television studio with the then BBC political editor Stephen Grimason and we were interviewed by Noel Thompson – another of those moments when some in the talks thought I should say nothing.

Days later there were news reports suggesting something more from the IRA – much more. If the sequence being negotiated as part of the Mitchell Review was accepted by the Ulster Unionist Council, then there would be a start to IRA decommissioning by the end of January 2000 and it would be completed within four months. I had heard nothing of this, knew nothing of this. It came out of the blue.

I called Martin McGuinness. Then I went to see him. I called him because of his position on the IRA Army Council, not that I would have said anything about that on the telephone. I asked him to put himself in my shoes. He gave me clear advice. Firstly, in our telephone conversation: 'If I was in your shoes, I would keep my nerve ... and, at the end of this process, you will be vindicated.' Then, in our meeting in the Carrickdale Hotel later, with Eamonn Mallie also present, he told us the immediate task was for politics to be seen to be working. And, in terms of any possible voluntary gestures on decommissioning, McGuinness pointed 'up the road'. Not now; not as a result of anything happening inside the Mitchell Review.

We had asked to see him after he had spoken at the annual republican commemorative march at Edentubber. We had a cup of tea and a biscuit together in the Carrickdale afterwards. I had also been speaking with others, including the P. O'Neill of this time, all of them telling me the same thing – that actual decommissioning was not being discussed by the IRA. But, given his rank, the words from McGuinness carried more weight, offered more certainty, allowed me to be more confident in the news assessments I was making.

Ulster Unionist Ken Maginnis was inside the Mitchell Review negotiation – seeing words being drafted, going between the negotiating teams, able to read the tea leaves from inside the cup. He told me that the timetable on decommissioning being reported was not on any piece of paper he had read. Days later, Maginnis would share some words with me from inside those talks, a confirmation that he was well informed.

Inside the BBC, I was speaking to Colman, briefing him on what I was being told. He kept his nerve and helped me keep mine. He could easily have told me to go quiet, say nothing, wait to see what developed. But he did none of that, did not pull me back, but, on air, allowed me to say what my sources were telling me. My speaking note for an interview with Wendy Austin on BBC *Good Morning Ulster* on 15 November 1999, includes:

> I simply pose this question. If there was certainty about a decommissioning process beginning in January and ending in May, why would unionists have so much difficulty with this deal? And, I think, people will know the answer to that question. Because if we are to believe that, from absolutely no decommissioning, we're going to head into a process where everything will be decommissioned within a four-month period, then the IRA is about to jump over the moon.

I was later told that Trimble was not happy with my 'over the moon' comment. I used it deliberately to emphasise the enormity of what was being suggested. I was thinking about every word. I had to in this moment. The NIO started calling after every interview I did – calling to explain the logic of devolution and decommissioning; that in the event of government, the question of guns would have to be answered. The IRA would have to respond. I was told I was 'wrong', was 'overstating knowledge', that I was being told 'downright lies' and that I should 'suspend judgement'. I kept talking. Thinking, yes, about these conversations, but placing more trust in the advice and information I had from McGuinness and Maginnis.

The Mitchell sequence started to run on 16 November, taking Trimble closer to that big step into the Executive. First, his party council had to meet. That was scheduled for later in the month. The first IRA statement, as part of these developments, was due on 17 November. Ken Maginnis gave me the words the day before, not to be used exactly, but to inform my reports. This is my Radio Ulster news script from 16 November 1999:

> The next development in a carefully choreographed sequence of events is expected to be a statement from the IRA. Sources are suggesting it will be brief and will confirm that the IRA leadership is appointing a representative to enter into discussions with the Canadian General John de Chastelain and his decommissioning body. The IRA statement will not respond to the unionist demand for it to say 'the war is over', but don't be surprised if it states a strong commitment to freedom, justice and peace. The IRA is expected to put on record its support for Sinn Féin, probably acknowledging the leadership the party has given during the peace process. In the past, the IRA has described the Good Friday Agreement as a significant development. That is likely to be repeated with the IRA possibly adding

that its full implementation will contribute to a lasting peace. Today, Sinn Féin spoke of the IRA's guns being silent. They will have to remain so if David Trimble is to have any chance of selling the deal on offer.

The next day, 17 November, in a meeting just after noon, P. O'Neill gave me the actual statement: 'Not that you need it,' he said. The statement was the identical twin of the information that Ken Maginnis had given me, thus confirming that the Unionist MP knew exactly what was going on inside these talks.

I was still wondering about the other information that was out there, this decommissioning timetable that had been reported. I asked a Special Branch source if it was their intelligence: 'No, no, no,' he replied. He thought that the possibility of the IRA leadership 'softening up' the organisation was 'a very long-term thing'. This was another way, I suppose, of saying what Martin McGuinness had said about possibilities 'up the road'. That road would be two years long, not the couple of months that Trimble was prepared to risk. That Executive lasted a short time. There were no calls from the NIO to tell me my analysis had been right. Their attempt to soundproof the talks and control the lines failed. Their assessment of the logic of what would happen was wrong.

What were the lessons in all of this? That a government will always try to control the news. For me, the personal learning was the importance of having a range of sources, seeing through the spin, checking and checking again. Also, the importance of having a strong editor and the need to share information with Andrew Colman to allow him to make his decisions. The IRA stretched the decommissioning elastic from a starting point of 'not a bullet–not an ounce', into a commentary about 'silent guns', then sealed bunkers and inspections, eventually agreeing a scheme with de Chastelain to put 'arms beyond use', and, then, a beginning in 2001 to 'save the peace process'. All of this was stretched through to 2005.

I found this period a nightmare – too much at times. The messengers in this place need bulletproof vests. Not literally, but you will understand what I mean. The government was telling unionists what they wanted to hear. First Trimble, then Ian Paisley and Peter Robinson. Much of it involved thinking about logical outcomes in a process not always determined or decided by logic. That, also, was a big part of the learning.

In this period, we were also seeing the flaws in peace, how long these processes take. We were understanding now, as we watched the various struggles, that politics becomes the next battle after war. At times it was infuriating. There are different interests and needs. We learned how important the issue of prisoners was for some of those in the negotiations; how important the question of decommissioning was for others. It involved understanding what McGuinness said about the need for politics to show it can work, that it can make a difference, that things will change. It also meant understanding Trimble's position: that decommissioning would be an important statement of a commitment to peace; that it was irreversible; that people could believe it and that, in those circumstances, politics could and would work so much better. It sounds easy, but it is not. The different sides in this had different concerns and issues to manage, and difficult people to manage – the non-believers on all sides: those who didn't trust Adams and McGuinness, and those who didn't trust Trimble and the 'Brits'. For all of the participants, these became the sleepless nights of peace, that restless turning and the questions: have we done the right thing? What if we have done the wrong thing?

# SEVEN

# Seeing Through the Fog

## *The 'Branch' still making the IRA family tree*

IT BECAME A DIFFERENT KIND of war; different in this sense – that the story was not being told in the headlines of bombs and bullets, but in the revelation of bugs and wires and in the stories of trespass into the most sensitive places of politics and intelligence. One part of the story was Special Branch and MI5 listening for a loose word and watching for a wrong move. And the other part was the IRA stepping into places of secrets that should have been well out of bounds to them. All of this was the cat-and-mouse of something which eventually broke the politics in the peace. When you have fought each other through so many years, it wasn't going to end in a hug, not in a place so small. In this period of the late 1990s and stretching into the new decade, there was still little or no trust. That other war of bombs and bullets was still too close. People had too much to remember and were not able, or not willing, to forget. A capitulation or a betrayal in the peace was as bad as in the war. It wasn't over – not yet, not by a long shot.

Reporting these intelligence battles had its challenges. Lies were offered as truth. The IRA denied involvement in certain events – not once but many times. Working relationships with that organisation broke down. Angry words were exchanged. As I thought about those arguments and allowed competing pieces of information to race through my head, there were nights when I didn't sleep. I relied on trusted colleagues for a second, third and fourth opinion. And I learned that the peace could be as messed up as the war, by which I mean the challenge of reporting it as I tried to sift out the disinformation.

The lack of trust between the sides – IRA and British – made its way into the headlines in big moments of news, including in the story of a bug concealed inside a car and discovered in late 1999. Our focus was still on the political negotiation of that time, the period I wrote about in the previous chapter. The bug was inside a car used by Adams and McGuinness and by the senior Belfast republican Martin Lynch. It was an intrusion into that top tier – the invisible passenger, if you like; a stranger travelling with the closest of friends. By being inside a car used by Adams, McGuinness and Lynch to travel to and from meetings with the IRA leadership during the talks of that time, the tracking and listening device was designed to pinpoint meeting places and to hear conversations from outside the talks. All of this was as important, indeed, arguably more important, than what was being said inside the negotiations.

At the time, Adams told us he had been in touch with

Downing Street and with the Taoiseach's Department. He wanted answers. He also spoke of the spooks and the spies still being at their work. Of course, they were. So, too, was the IRA intelligence team and its 'director' Bobby Storey. On a stage behind the politics, such revelations would on occasion create moments of drama, then of crisis – a confirmation that not all of the war was over.

I have dug deeper into that intelligence war. It was a reminder that, at that time, the IRA had not ended its armed campaign, and that, inside the intelligence community, Special Branch was still monitoring this vast organisational structure – its enemy. I learned of something called an 'ORBAT' (order of battle) analysis. It was an intelligence assessment that attempted to piece together the shape of the IRA through its ranks, from top to bottom; an assessment that added names to the roles across that frame – from the Army Council to the General Headquarters Staff, through finance, overseas procurements, adjutant roles, quartermaster roles, IRA engineering roles, to those responsible for 'mainland' operations, internal security, explosives officers, and those tasked with restructuring the organisation, with intelligence and with training (in this period a woman's name appears in that role). Then, it drills down into the specific make-up of active service units. Alongside names, Special Branch then added a number to each individual who appeared in their intelligence assessment of the IRA. The contacts and associates of those people were also logged and given numbers. The numbers and names then became the pieces in the jigsaw puzzle; how Special Branch built the IRA picture, but never all of it. There were always missing numbers and missing pieces – the blind corners on which intelligence can crash.

These assessments were still happening beyond the period of the Belfast/Good Friday Agreement and its implementation through the Mitchell Review, with still five years or so to go before the IRA would end its war. It is important context in relation to that developing political and peace story. It illuminates what had happened and what had not yet happened – a context in which not just the spooks and spies were still at their work, but, also, the IRA. Surely Adams would have known that.

Those ORBAT and other assessments had all the names you would expect in IRA leadership roles, including Bobby Storey as director of intelligence but also with a role in the 'mainland/overseas' department, along with another prominent west Belfast republican and one of the organisation's leaders in south Armagh. But the reach of the assessment was much more than the obvious and headline names, and it gives us an idea of the breadth and depth of the intelligence effort as we moved into the year 2000 and beyond – dozens of names and some nicknames well known inside the republican circle, but not outside it. The 'Branch' was still piecing together the IRA family tree, connecting the links and the lines, the names and the numbers. As I consider the extent of that knowledge in relation to the IRA, I have questions about what happened next.

There are two stories, just months apart. The first was on a Sunday night in March 2002, St Patrick's Day, when the IRA walked in the corridors of its enemy. Think of those steps behind the lines and the documents that were stolen from a Special Branch office. Remarkably, there was nothing on camera – they were not recording, asleep in the peace. That Sunday night, Castlereagh police headquarters in Belfast was a place of calm, then confusion and finally chaos. Why was it wide open? So easily accessed? Was there a sense that they, the IRA, wouldn't dare? Or, like the security cameras at that base, had people just dropped their guard? When I think about it now, it beggars belief that an intrusion of this type, into such a sensitive place of secrets and intelligence, would or should be so simple. This walking in and walking out without challenge. As is the case with so much of the 'war', we don't have the whole story of Castlereagh. What we do know is that as a result of the break-in agents/sources were compromised as the IRA began to decode the documents.

Within a few months, things moved to another scene, in another part of the city. Special Branch and MI5 were running a covert operation, and intelligence officers were inside a house in west Belfast. They had a key, which they had used many times, part of what they call 'alternative means of entry'. I am told there was panic in the house when those involved in that covert operation were told that the owner was nearby, returning unexpectedly. He was missed in the surveillance operation as he left his girlfriend's home.

A bag and documents were upstairs under a bed. These

documents, including some taken from inside the NIO, were hidden in what the IRA would have considered a safe house. This operation had run through several months. MI5 and Special Branch knew the IRA had stolen the documents and where they were, and they were waiting for the right moment to make arrests – waiting for one man in particular. This all became part of the story that was given the name Stormontgate.

These things represented a continuation of the war games. In that time, there was still a need to know your enemy. I remember the shock when the IRA was linked to the break-in at Castlereagh. Then, months later, more shock as that political intelligence-gathering episode of Stormontgate was brought to our attention. This is when I would hear Bobby Storey's name time and time again. There was less shock about the continuing bugging operations targeting senior republicans, their cars, their conversations, their homes and their offices. Yet, war is that two-way thing; intelligence-gathering a game of sides, with each side needing to field its best team in an effort to stay on top.

The list of codenames (of agents/sources) stolen from the Castlereagh police base would have given the IRA some indication at least of the continuing surveillance and information-gathering efforts of Special Branch. They also had the names of the agents' handlers and their telephone numbers, as well as details of what Special Branch would log as addresses of interest and people of interest. These were the 'sparkling diamonds', if not the 'crown jewels'. The actual names of the agents were not in room 220 at Castlereagh, but concealed beneath other layers of security, inside the 'source unit', since moved and renamed the 'intelligence centre'.

Years later, breaking ranks and breaking silence, a one-time senior figure in the IRA told me of their efforts to decode the documents, trying to work out this 'Castlereagh stuff'. His first contact with me was through a third party. After that I had a conversation with him, then a first face-to-face meeting. 'Every codename on the Castlereagh file had a relevance,' he told me. He mentioned Roy McShane as one of those outed as a result of the Castlereagh information. McShane ran from Belfast in February 2008. I would have spoken to him many times: 'Hello!' Perhaps a word or two about golf. I can still see him standing in my company. He was known to journalists, known because of his role as a driver – the man who often would have been in the car with Adams and other republican leaders, with them when they arrived for news conferences or at the various media offices in Belfast for interviews. He was always busy, but always had time for a word. The day after he ran, I was quoted in the *Belfast Telegraph*:

> He may just have been part of a pool of drivers, but he was driving the most significant figures in the republican leadership, including Gerry Adams and Martin McGuinness. He would have known where they were going and who they were seeing at particular times and all of that goes into a wider frame. So, Denis

Donaldson was in the office, Roy McShane was in the car and other agents are in different places and the information they all provide makes the bigger picture.

In my conversations with that former senior IRA figure, he told me: 'The information the IRA got out of that place [Castlereagh] is frightening.' He was speaking to me in a house in Belfast, where we met on two occasions. That description of the Castlereagh material as 'frightening' reminded me of something that the loyalist David Ervine said in 2002, at the time of the break-in, and just after he had met with then Northern Ireland Secretary of State Dr John Reid. Ervine told me that Reid's biggest fear was, 'Do they [the IRA] know what they have?' By the time I met that former senior IRA figure years later, that organisation had had plenty of time to work it out. My source described an argument in the Short Strand in east Belfast between the IRA 'adjutant', who was a member of the Army Council, and a dissident republican. He told me the adjutant 'blabbed out' the dissident's 'codename and number'. This was the outworking of the 'Castlereagh stuff' – the IRA knowing what it had, knowing how to use it, knowing how cutting and how damaging such an accusation would be when spoken and heard inside the republican community. I know who that dissident is, but 2015 was the first time I had heard the detail of that row. Then I started to join it up with another piece of information.

There had been a letter addressed to me and posted to the *Belfast Telegraph* five years earlier. The postmark on the envelope is 26.02.10. Inside, eight paragraphs had been typed on an A4 page: codenames, some numbers and the name of that dissident republican who had been confronted in the Short Strand – his actual name, no codename or number. He was named, alongside two others, and described as 'ours', meaning agents. The opening paragraph in the letter read: 'As a former Special Branch Officer in the Royal Ulster Constabulary I cannot remain silent any longer. I gave long years of loyal service. I lost good friends and colleagues, for what?' It closed with these sentences: 'I served in Special Branch. I know what I am talking about. Why am I writing to you? Because someone needs to ask the questions. The protection of agents seems to outweigh the protection of the public. This cannot be allowed to continue.'

In how it was constructed, the letter suggested it was written by someone who knew the police intelligence system. My notebook from the time walks me through the chronology of what I did. On 4 March 2010 I spoke with someone at police headquarters. The police were interested in the letter. That day, two officers came to see me in the offices of the *Belfast Telegraph*. One of them was from Intelligence Branch (C3). By now, I had photocopied the letter and the envelope. I knew they would want the originals. The following day, 5 March 2010, I went to see a retired officer, someone who would know that intelligence system. His assessment was that the letter was 'not a hoax'; that the number format used within it was 'how CHIS [covert human intelligence sources] are registered'. He told me the author had knowledge, was 'disgruntled' to the point of putting lives at risk – whether the information was right or wrong.

An operational name was also included in the letter, which police asked us not to use. No one was telling us it was 'balls' or the work of a 'fantasist'. The newspaper ran the story on 6 March 2010. Before it did, it emerged the letter had also been sent to then crime correspondent Deborah McAleese.

My opening paragraph in the coverage read: 'PSNI detectives have begun an investigation into what could prove to be a life-threatening leak of intelligence secrets.' The report included these lines from the Police Service of Northern Ireland (PSNI): 'We do not comment on intelligence matters. However, we can confirm that an investigation has already commenced into an alleged leak of sensitive information to a media source.' Had they had no concerns, there would have been no investigation and no statement to the newspaper. There would have been no story and the letter would have ended up in the bin.

More recently, I sought another opinion on the letter from someone who would know. There was confirmation of some, but not all of the detail. On the three dissidents identified as 'ours', meaning Special Branch sources, the response was: 'Yes, yes, yes.' There was confirmation also of the detail of the intelligence operation that the newspaper had been asked not to publish in 2010. Whoever wrote that letter had inside knowledge or information.

Having thought back to that letter in 2010, I then thought forward to those 2015 meetings and conversations with that one-time senior IRA figure – to those contacts and meetings that came out of the blue. And, inside my head, I then had a different question about that anonymous correspondence. Could the IRA have sent it? Was this them using the 'Castlereagh stuff'? Was it outrageous to even consider that possibility? Did the information in the letter go beyond what was taken from Castlereagh during that break-in of 2002? These stories never end. They develop over time. They can change. I asked the question but got nowhere with it. But it is an example of how you find yourself in the crossfire and the cross-play of these intelligence games – how you can get lost in them; think one thing, then another. It works inside your head – always questions. Not being able to see all the strings and those playing or pulling them.

Going back to 2002, to the time of the break-in and the earthquake of that moment, the IRA, including in meetings with me and in briefings read to me, denied involvement. These were P. O'Neill contacts – from the top. And there were other conversations with other republicans. There were statements from Sinn Féin as well. Of course, they denied it. Imagine the political fallout from a statement by the IRA in March 2002 saying, 'We did it.' In their thinking, I suppose, this was their permissible lie, one of several in this period. Bobby Storey was arrested and released in 2002, but in my notes of that period, I find his name everywhere, both in relation to Castlereagh and then the Stormontgate story. On the Castlereagh job, a senior Special Branch officer told me: 'It's Provos. It's Bobby Storey's team. This is an act of war. They've got a lot of stuff. They have the whole Belfast Department [Special Branch]. Contact numbers. Names. Not addresses.' Then on the Stormontgate intelligence-gathering episode, a line is repeated: 'It's the Storey team.' Then, from another Special Branch source: 'It seems a huge risk for the organisation [IRA] to take, and it has blown up in their face.'

The IRA denials were not credible, nor were the lines from other republicans or the statements from Sinn Féin. The scale of the denial was something else. There was a statement from Gerry Kelly on 16 April that he was 'absolutely satisfied' that the IRA was not involved. Five days later, I had a P. O'Neill briefing face to face in west Belfast. I scribbled it on three BBC taxi vouchers, including these lines:

- The ceasefire remains intact.
- The IRA is no threat to the peace process.
- The IRA did not carry out Castlereagh.
- Some section of British Intelligence did carry it out.

I reported that briefing, alongside lines from security sources that IRA intelligence-gathering was being kept up to date and that these sources were linking the IRA to the Castlereagh robbery. The acting Chief Constable, Colin Cramphorn, said IRA involvement in the break-in was a major line of inquiry.

Then, the next phone call was from someone close to Adams. I have a comment logged from a conversation on 22 April 2002, a little over a month after the break-in at Special Branch offices: 'There are people in the Brit system trying to create a crisis. There is a view that you are being used.' More mind games; more of the play – this suggestion of the 'Brits' using me to throw their stones, their muck, to do their damage. I found it all quite insulting. The republican/ IRA denial in this story did not add up. We were heading towards a breakdown, if that is the right way to describe it. It came just months later, when I ran detailed news reports on the IRA developing weapons in Colombia and the level of leadership clearance that had been given inside the organisation for that to happen. The information was from an intelligence assessment. I had asked to interview the IRA. There was silence until the day of our coverage on 13 June.

A week earlier that source close to Adams told me there was 'no evidence' for my report. That line of a few months earlier, that I was being used, was repeated. I was told if I ran the report I would be 'finished with republicans'. 'This will start a bushfire that could end in an inferno,' he said. Hours before that news report, I had another face-to-face meeting with P. O'Neill. It was terse. Blunt. A repeat of that line that I was being used. There was talk of the final nail in the coffin for the Good Friday Agreement; then two follow-up telephone calls to emphasise the points in the earlier meeting. The news reports ran. Silence followed. P. O'Neill and other republicans slammed the door – for now, at least. Months later, as the Stormontgate news broke, politics fell into a deep sleep. Stormont was no longer sustainable in such circumstances.

In these testing and unnerving moments, you learn to hold your line. The IRA denials didn't stack up. Had it breached the security of Special Branch in wartime, stolen their secrets, there would have been a statement of many lines, but not in the peace. They had to keep it to themselves, share it in circles that they considered to be secure. This was the Storey team and the Storey way. Then, when we get to the Colombian story, am I surprised that P. O'Neill tried to shut me up, then shut me down? No. In the developing peace, this became part of a wider pattern, like the LVF statement of 1999 and the NIO calls after my interviews during the Mitchell Review.

These things grind you down. Then they pass. They are arguments and stand-offs in the pressure of particular political moments, things you have to factor in until they are factored out. Then, years later, I heard the things I was told in those 2015 conversations – about the IRA efforts to decode the material and how they used it. Where do these lies in the peace fit within any truth process? And, as that wider intelligence piece is pulled more and more into the public place and conversation, how will the story of agents look? What might have seemed right in the decision-making of that conflict period will look very different and very wrong in the peace of now. They are, of course, two very different places and two very different contexts. They are not the same. Yet it is without that context that the ugliness and the darkness of that 'dirty war' is often held under a light.

Think about running agents or sources throughout

much of the conflict period. How different the world of communications was then: no mobile phones, no WhatsApp, no text messages or email. It was a context of limited contact, occasional meetings, snatched conversations, in which bits of a story would be heard, of someone's part involvement in some plan or action; in circumstances, described by one source, when 'fact and supposition tended to bleed into one another when being recounted'. The point he is making is that 'intelligence' in such moments becomes an agent's or a source's 'own interpretation'. The challenge then is trying to make sense of these fragments of information, knowing that what you have is far from the whole story. How fallible you are in such circumstances. This is not a world of perfect vision, or of such precision.

It is not just about what we think now, but about what others had to consider and contend with then. In the words of one source, it is a handler having to recognise 'the reality of the world to which their agent returned'; to places where a wrong word or a wrong question could be fatal; places where changes in routine are noticed; and places in which sightings with strangers are instantly recognised. As with the intelligence community, the IRA and loyalist organisations operated a 'convention of secrecy', worked on a 'need-to-know' basis. Agents who were part of these organisations took their orders from within, not from handlers. So, they would know about their part, their role in the different plans and actions, but not about the tasks assigned to others. And, they would also have known not to ask questions beyond their specific orders. People being too inquisitive, too nosey, were also noticed, more easily found out.

'It was mostly by listening and observing that the best agents acquired their knowledge and escaped suspicion.' This thinking is from an experienced senior figure in that intelligence community, now retired. 'Any view that an agent can be so controlled or directed or that he has the capacity to alter his paramilitary environment at will is a dangerous and misleading assumption.' Is this thinking something that we factor in when we look back from now – look back into the madness of then? Do we, to quote that retired intelligence officer, 'give due cognisance to the very unique set of circumstances that a state of endemic armed conflict and its accompanying acts of terrorism posed for the Government and its intelligence services, seeking to effectively protect its citizens from the horrific effects of the same'?

That 'intelligence war against terrorism' was not accompanied by the legal framework or the political accountability mechanisms of today. Yet it is judged by today's standards with fears that Whitehall will walk away and leave those here who fought that war to carry the can and the charge of collusion. These thoughts from inside that intelligence community are part of the context, but not all of the story.

I want to go back to January 1993, to an interview I did with one of the British generals, the late Sir John Wilsey. I was later told the story of a comment he is said to have made as he left Northern Ireland soon afterwards, at the end of his tour. As it was told to me, it was a throw-away line, a joking reference, about wishing he had never met two Brians: Nelson and Rowan. I interviewed the General Officer Commanding (GOC) at Thiepval Barracks in Lisburn. It was a big deal then – the first such interview with a general in a very long time. Nelson, the army agent operating inside the UDA, had been jailed, convicted of five counts of conspiracy to murder. He was different from other agents, in that he was picked and planted inside the UDA with the specific task of sharpening that organisation's intelligence. My question to Wilsey was a banana skin, one that, in his army boots, he stood on. I asked him, had the army felt shame? 'Certainly not ashamed,' he replied. The follow-up headlines told the story of what I considered then to be the foolishness of that answer. 'Fury over GOC stand on Nelson spy affair', 'Army chief in North is slammed over agent' and 'Blind eye to Nelson'. Wilsey said: 'If the Nelson episode taught us anything, it taught us that the relationship between the army and the RUC and other agencies involved was strong enough to withstand any pressures that came about because of that investigation.'

I have thought about that Wilsey answer many times since, understanding now a bit more of the background context – more than I would have known in 1993. At the time, I thought, how crass – a typical jingoistic general: uncaring, unapologetic, unthinking. But, in the course of any conflict, you learn as you go along. One of the things I know now that I did not know then was that in the late 1980s the Thatcher government had set, as its main military objective, the destruction of the IRA. Within that, there was no hint of talks or negotiation. So, think of how an order like that would play in the heads of soldiers. Wilsey probably thought he was doing his job, following orders. And, in those circumstances, why would he apologise? None of this is to excuse Nelson's actions. They are inexcusable. But when you give soldiers orders to destroy something, that is what they will do.

Nelson's activities were an expression and a confirmation of something very wrong, something rotten – a story that seemed unthinkable, unbelievable, and yet it was very real. The agent had what looked like participating rights, full membership of the war, if you like. It is hard to tell the difference between his army role and his UDA intelligence-gathering role. One seemed to complement the other. They were indistinguishable. There were no rules, no boundaries, no accountability, and, to quote the general, no shame. In a journal, Nelson wrote of a 'moral dilemma':

> Just how efficient would I make this intelligence network for the UDA ... Where does one draw the line? If I made it too efficient, I would be in trouble with BMI [British Military Intelligence]. Not efficient enough or lacking, and I would be in trouble with the UDA ... The only solution to the problem would be to try and meet both ends in the middle, which was easier said than done.

'Where's the line?' This question was posed by the veteran BBC *Panorama* reporter John Ware. He was talking about the line in the intelligence war, oftentimes blurred, sometimes invisible – the line that is the focus in so much of our conversation about truth, that Holy Grail that I described earlier. In his reporting during the conflict period here, Ware met Nelson on a number of occasions. 'He loved the sneaky-beaky stuff, the intrigue, knowing stuff that others didn't know.' Ware then describes Nelson's world – how he 'got a kick out of it', yet was 'permanently on edge'. Wiry. Taut. Chain-smoking cigarettes in the shadows of our war.

What if an outside investigator had not found him inside the UDA? Would his activities have continued? Was that the norm of then? The army tried to justify/explain their agent with a story of the scores of lives he saved. The numbers were greatly exaggerated – part of a made-up script; the opposite of truth. I saw him inside Crumlin Road Gaol. Passed him as I was being walked through the prison on a day when I was there for some other news story. He was polishing a floor in an isolation unit where he was being held – alone now, for his own safety. His job done, whatever that was. There was plenty of time in the early 1990s for him to work it out, to write that journal, his side of the story. It's a story that leaves others in that intelligence community with many questions. Then he disappeared – left Belfast. He is dead now. The army was not ashamed. There is a suggestion they gave him a medal. If they did, then the ugliness of this war was pinned on his lapel. How high did it go? How low did it go?

# EIGHT

# Face to Face with Freddie

## *Stakeknife and the Dirty War*

14 MAY 2003: THERE IS ALWAYS a surprise in the news of this place – even when you think there can be no more surprises. On this date, I sat in a room with Freddie Scappaticci, the last man I expected to see in Belfast on this day or on any other day. The talk was that he had run – chased by headlines, calling him names, names that in his community cut deep and are rarely forgiven. Usually, you end up dead. More than anyone else, he would have known the consequences of this. The story had exploded a few days earlier in the Sunday newspapers: the outing of an agent – decoding Stakeknife and finding Scappaticci. Could he really be back? Would he be that foolish? This was something more of a shock than a surprise. Not just that he was back, but that, over a cup of tea, I was being given arrangements for a possible meeting later that afternoon, in the heart of the republican community. A

meeting with Fred on the Falls. What was going on? Behind the scenes, there were many watching this play.

Scappaticci was allowed to live. For some reason, the republican leadership was willing to acquiesce in his denial that he had been a British agent. This would become the story of that date and that day: Freddie's escape; a tunnel away from those headlines and those names; his way out. Others were not afforded such doubt or such mercy. Those whose bodies were dumped for all to see, including those I saw on the border in the summer of 1992: interrogation, then execution. This was the way of the IRA court and its death penalty. But not for Scappaticci.

My meeting with him was controlled by others. He read a statement denying reports that he was the agent Stakeknife. They were scripted lines on a page. I managed to ask a few questions before his solicitor intervened to end the meeting. And I have since found out that there were others in the building. That republicans were managing Freddie's exit from the headlines, trying to get it over and done with. But nothing happens that quickly, not in this place, not in a story of this kind. It's still running. Freddie is still running. And, to quote a source, republicans are 'tainted' by their involvement in that escape.

An investigation team from outside Northern Ireland is probing Stakeknife: the story of an army agent inside the IRA internal security team, the department that, in the war, combed and culled that organisation, hunting down the 'touts' and the 'informers'. One agent was involved in the torture and the questioning of other suspected agents, leaving those in the intelligence world open to the charge of 'playing God', something they dispute and reject as suiting or fitting a particular point of view or narrative. In 2012 Sir John Wilsey, whom I referenced in the previous chapter, confirmed the role of Scappaticci. He did so while speaking to a military intelligence whistleblower posing as a television researcher. The former Commander of UK Land Forces was recorded describing Stakeknife as the military's 'most important secret'. 'It was the golden egg. It was the one thing that was terribly, terribly important to the army ... So, we were terribly cagey about Fred.' There you have it: the 'golden egg'.

What a description of a man in such a role: the interrogator of other suspected agents. It suggests a ruleless war, not clueless, because we have to believe that in the brains of intelligence all of this was part of the calculation, part of that collateral damage – the working out of what is important and who is more important; that some agents have a shelf-life because others are better placed to provide better information. And, in this case, that some have higher access within the IRA. Is that what really happened? How blind people became.

Almost twenty years after his comments about Brian Nelson, the same general had now marched into another intelligence controversy, this time the Stakeknife story. Fred was back in the headlines: 'Taped call gives Stakeknife Insight'; 'Scappaticci was our most prized agent during the Troubles: Army chief'; 'Army is accused of "perverse" war games';

155

'Finally, there is nowhere left to hide for Scappaticci'.

To tell this story I want to retrace my steps. Go back to 2003. It was Saturday evening, 10 May. News began to emerge that the *Sunday People* would name the agent Stakeknife, the first time that Scappaticci would be attached or linked to that codename. That evening, I called a former senior Special Branch officer, who confirmed the name and the role Scappaticci had inside the IRA, at the heart of its internal security department. The officer told me something more: that Special Branch believed Scappaticci had been involved in the killings of 'a number of our people', meaning Special Branch agents inside the IRA. And he asked a question: Did the army allow it?

As the story developed in those hours into Sunday, there was confusion as to whether Scappaticci had left Northern Ireland. On Sunday morning, a republican told me that somebody had seen him the night before with his grandchild. Guidance that would follow in other conversations described Stakeknife as having worked 'historically'. In other words, the role was not current. I was told: 'He is refusing to go.' Refusing to leave Northern Ireland. 'There is no problem with the name,' a PSNI source said. 'The problem is how many people have that name' – a couple of sentences that confirmed Scappaticci as 'Stakeknife' but expressed concern that his name was now in wide circulation adding significantly to the danger he faced. Later, on Sunday, I was told, 'He's now gone,' meaning he had listened to advice and left. Gone to where, I didn't know.

This was my script for my Radio Ulster news report at midnight:

> For some years there has been speculation about the identity of 'Stakeknife'. And now the army's agent has been unmasked. The Sunday newspapers named him as Freddie Scappaticci, and security sources have confirmed that he has now left Northern Ireland. On Friday, in the knowledge that he was about to be publicly identified, he was warned that his personal security was compromised. But there were reports that he was seen in Belfast during the weekend and that he was refusing to move. Stakeknife has since been persuaded to leave. The Stevens Team plan to interview the agent. There are allegations that he was involved in a number of murders, including the killing of other agents. And Sir John Stevens will want to establish how much the Army knew. Stakeknife is not someone who would be known on the public stage. But security sources say he was a 'significant IRA figure' and 'very effective' in the intelligence world. There are suggestions that in recent years the agent had become dormant and was no longer a source of significant intelligence on the IRA.

How could you possibly justify such an agent? It is 2021 now, and I am speaking to a long-time intelligence officer, now retired: 'A moral conundrum that could be debated at length,' was part of his response:

Do you take on such an individual especially when [he] is volunteering to work for you, but knowing the nature of the work the security team in any paramilitary organisation was commissioned to do? In that respect you are being offered unique access to a substantial degree into the upper echelons of the godfathers of the organisation and to learn of their fears, plans and paramilitary objectives, but at the same time engaging with an individual whose role was in effect to be an interrogator/executioner of those suspected to have betrayed the cause. Hard choice to make, walk away consoling yourself that it is morally and ethically the right thing to do, but in doing so rendering yourself blind to a flow of information that no other source could produce. We cannot overlook the information produced by Stakeknife that did save lives, but I suspect the focus will be on the lives not saved even if any attempt to do so would have quickly rendered the source at great peril for his own life.

On the wider question of the 'intelligence war' and the use of agents, he then offered another challenge: 'To see things from another perspective, where a war, if not in name, was being fought, and the ethical and moral fog which surrounded the whole world of intelligence-gathering in a democracy.' This officer had nothing to do with recruiting or handling Stakeknife. He was offering an opinion, no more than that;

responding to my question; knowing, of course, that there are no easy or simple answers.

Back in May 2003, my meeting with Scappaticci did not just happen. It was made to happen. It was part of a plan. It was Wednesday now. There would have been time for him to think about those headlines, the content of those news reports, to get his lines right with others. I wondered what he would look like. Would he be nervous? I was. How would he try to explain himself? In those few days since the weekend headlines, he would have had time to speak with people in the intelligence world; time to try to think straight, to assess the risk of returning to Belfast, where he would have known that the IRA would want to talk to him. That weekend coverage brought more of us into his story. More than that, it made us think again of days in the war. It was a read back to those pages of interrogation and execution that were part of the script then; a thinking back to some of the IRA statements, some of the lines – how cold they were, how ruthless. In one case, dating back into the 1980s, there were these words: 'We are not prepared to state how we eventually detected him, but clearly the RUC are lying when they stated that Joseph Fenton had no connections with them ... We realise the predicament that this places the Fenton family circle [in]. They cannot be held responsible for Joseph Fenton and should bear no stigma for his actions.' The torture doesn't end with the 'collaborator'. Whatever the words of the IRA, it extends to the family, into communities within which there is little or no forgiveness for this.

I remember going to the Fenton family home; a young lad running towards me, someone getting hold of him, me being told politely that no one had anything to say, then leaving. I could walk away. Others are left in the mess of that 'dirty war' – left to deal with its consequences.

When you look back into this world, into those times, you think also of the last letters written to families. Then, you start to think about this man, Stakeknife, and you go deeper than you intend, imagining those settings, his part in the interrogations – the fear, the terror, the finality, walls closing in ... claustrophobic ... no escape. I think about someone trying to hold a pen, writing, composing words in such hopeless circumstances. Then there are the tapes that were made, tapes on which, I am told, you can hear a clinking sound of a spoon on a glass – the signal to start talking after the record button has been pressed. This, the confession. Closer now to death. How much do these people tell before the bullet is fired? What is done to make them talk? The torture – mental and physical; little hope of being rescued. For too many, this is the risk and the reality of a dirty war, with no way out.

In the middle of all of this grotesqueness, the army had an agent – Stakeknife ... Scappaticci. Not tied to some chair, not hooded or pleading or begging for mercy, not one of those with a pen in his shaking hand or talking into a tape recorder. But, instead, running the show, conducting the interrogations. Soon, I would be face to face with this man; face to face with Freddie, a solicitor by his side and with a prepared statement – a statement that represented a door being left open, a way to get out of this mess, out of the headlines. The IRA may not have believed him but, for now, they were prepared to accept his denial. He was too much trouble, too big an embarrassment to be executed, because that would be a confirmation of his role, which would then ask questions of others higher up in the IRA. How the army, how the 'Brits', got inside their internal security department. How do you even begin to explain that?

That date – 14 May 2003 – was one of those complicated days, when you have to go along with the various acts in the play – one meeting; another meeting. The first was in west Belfast just after noon, at which I was told that Scappaticci may have something to say later. I would need a camera. There was a question also about sharing the pictures with other news outlets. I needed to speak to Andrew Colman, the Head of News at the BBC in Belfast, explain to him what was happening. I would do that and call as soon as I had. I spoke with Colman and another colleague, David Lynas, the news organiser, who arranged a crew for me. They were the only two in the BBC who knew where I was going and who I was going to see. Then I travelled with the cameraman, Sam Wilson, to a designated waiting point. We arrived before two and waited for an hour or so. Another journalist, Anne Cadwallader, was also there. Then we got the phone call, to come to an office on the Falls Road, within walking distance of where we were.

As the solicitor, Michael Flanigan, was speaking with

us, there was an unscripted moment, something that was not a part of the plan – two other journalists at the door, asking for Flanigan, colleagues of mine at the BBC working for the *Spotlight* programme, Vincent Kearney and Brendan McCourt. Had I told them? No, I hadn't. I would learn later that they were following up the weekend reports and a statement from Flanigan the previous day. Their timing was a coincidence. But what a coincidence. They were told that Flanigan was unavailable. Minutes later, Freddie entered the room. This man of headlines, in short sleeves and with a prepared script for this moment. There were to be no questions, but I managed to ask a few before being closed down. He looked nervous but didn't sound nervous.

Rowan: Why do you think this label 'Stakeknife' has been attached to you?

Scappaticci: I don't know.

Rowan: Were you aware of this at all before the weekend publication?

Scappaticci: No. I became aware of it on Saturday night.

Rowan: And just one final question. Your statement has said, the statement yesterday and it's repeated today, that you're not Stakeknife. Were you at any stage a member of the IRA and involved in the republican movement?

Scappaticci: (pause) Ummmm. I was involved in the
republican movement thirteen years ago. But have
[had] no involvement this past thirteen years.

I would have had a hundred questions for him, but that
wasn't going to be allowed. To ask one was a battle. Two
was stretching it. And I knew, from the body language of
his solicitor, that the third would be my last. You may think
that Scappaticci said nothing in those replies, but he said
something – something significant – hidden in those few
words. That third question and answer delivered a Columbo-
type moment. That reply about no involvement in the
republican movement this past thirteen years: he didn't say
it, but that answer took us back to 1990, when the IRA stood
down the Scappaticci security team; stood it down after the
cavalry came charging in to rescue a suspected informer
from an IRA interrogation at a house in west Belfast.

That time, unlike so many other times, there was to be no
execution. Instead, a news conference was to be held, where
the informer Sandy Lynch would expose Special Branch.
Danny Morrison, then Sinn Féin's publicity director, was
sent for. We now know that he was being walked into a trap.
As he arrived, police and soldiers came running. Morrison,
trying to escape the scene, was arrested in a neighbouring
house. What a scalp for the security forces – one of the most
senior figures in the republican leadership, its man of words,
a public face, close to Adams. Morrison believes he was 'set
up' by Scappaticci and his handlers: 'I think, at some stage,

it became a very attractive option, but I don't know when.' Morrison was speaking to me some years ago. 'Sandy Lynch, in court, gave evidence that it was Scappaticci who put to him that idea of doing a news conference. I was sent for on the Sunday afternoon. As soon as I went through the front door [of the house where Lynch was being held], the cavalry arrived.' Stakeknife had delivered a considerable prize. Years later, Morrison's conviction for the false imprisonment of Lynch was quashed. No reason was given and he was denied access to pertinent information on the grounds that it was confidential. Morrison believes it was part of covering up the Stakeknife story.

Back at the BBC, they were waiting for me. Andrew Colman had gathered the editors. The pictures of that brief meeting with Scappaticci would soon be the lead story, inside the BBC and outside – the statements that were read, the few words he spoke in reply to my questions, his denial of the Stakeknife allegation. But, also, my words, quoting security sources. I was in studio with the BBC presenter Noel Thompson, I think in a borrowed jacket and tie. I had not been expecting this news day and its developments. Not for one minute did I think I would ever be in the same room as Freddie. I spoke to Noel about hearing two very different stories: 'What we got from Mr Scappaticci today was a very categoric, firm denial of all of the allegations that have been made ... [but] I'm being told by security sources that the agent known as Stakeknife is a man called Freddie Scappaticci and a man in his late fifties. That's what they have been telling us.'

I told him that information had not been withdrawn, and I made another point, that: 'When I was on my way to west Belfast today to see him, and this was probably a couple of hours before the actual interview happened, I got a call from a security source who told me that there was the prospect of this man making a public appearance ... They knew it was coming.'

That call was from the Director of Communications at the PSNI, Austin Hunter. So, the story was not just about what Freddie said, but, more importantly, the confirmation from security sources that Scappaticci was 'Stakeknife'. That the police also knew he was about to appear in public told us how closely they were watching his movements. The following day, a republican, whom I had met those twenty-four hours earlier as part of the sequence leading to the Scappaticci meeting, called me to complain about my reports. It was an indication of how they were trying to control things, just how nervous they were in this moment. They wanted the prepared lines, not any questioning of the Scappaticci script. But that is not the way news works. Not in war. Not in peace.

As agreed, the BBC shared the material from that news conference on 14 May 2003. Freddie's face was now everywhere, including in the newspaper coverage the next day. The headlines were asking their own questions. On the front page of *The Guardian*: 'Identity parade. This man says he isn't Stakeknife, and has never left Ulster. Just what is going on?' What was going on was a play, a bluff, a game. Fred, having weighed up his options, was taking a chance. *The Irish Times* went with: 'Scappaticci appears in public to deny he is "Stakeknife"'. *The Daily Telegraph*: 'Stakeknife suspect in dramatic TV appearance'. *The Irish News*: 'Scappaticci emerges from hiding to deny he was a mole'. And *The Independent*: 'In short sleeves and spectacles, Scappaticci steps out of shadows to insist: I'm no IRA spy'.

Under the last of those headlines, the paper's acclaimed Ireland Correspondent David McKittrick, wrote:

> Freddie Scappaticci, a barrel-chested man in a short-sleeved shirt, yesterday stepped from the shadows to deny that he was the infamous Stakeknife, the Army secret agent at the heart of the IRA. He did so at the west Belfast offices of his solicitor, confounding those who thought he had been spirited away to Britain by the authorities to escape a vengeful IRA. His appearance is the latest twist in the tale of Stakeknife, one of the Army's most valuable informers, which gained impetus at the weekend when Mr Scappaticci was named as the agent by newspapers. His denials yesterday were comprehensive. In a filmed interview with two Belfast journalists, Brian Rowan of the BBC and a freelance, Anne Cadwallader, he declared: 'I am not guilty of any of these allegations. I have not left Northern Ireland since I was challenged by reporters on Saturday night. Nobody has had the decency to ask me if any of these allegations were true.'

Scappaticci spoke of 'decency'. But you find nothing decent when you dig deep into his role and shovel up and shovel out the different layers of that dirty war in which he was a significant player. Nothing decent, when you read back into the statements of the interrogations and the confessions, and you think again of him as an agent in those settings and those scenes that we don't really want to imagine. Yet, we are made to think about them: the detail; what was said by the IRA; how callous war is; how contemptible its various plays; how confusing. I wonder about what the army thinks, about the bodies, about the words in the statements, about their man in the middle of this. What code of war or ethics allowed it? What thinking took them to this point? What set of rules or principles? Or did people just get lost in that ethical and moral fog? It was wrong from its starting point. They understood his role. There can be no talk of not knowing. I also wonder what Scappaticci thought then and thinks now. Decency? There is nothing in the definition of that word that could be attached to his part in those dark places from where he presented people for execution.

The IRA was part of what happened on that day in May 2003. Bobby Storey was outside the building, seen by my colleagues who had called to the office hoping to speak with Michael Flanigan. And, years later, I would learn of other republicans being inside those offices as Scappaticci spoke with us. A source with inside knowledge told me that it would be safe to say that Scappaticci was in close contact with the republican leadership before that news event, that his denial suited the leadership, who had decided to go along with it and deal with it later down the road. This conversation was in December 2016. It was another reminder of what you see and don't see in actual time. The IRA was part of the working-out of that day, a day when others were watching and listening.

Many years later, a colleague asked me was this a day when all eyes were on me? I said it was a day when all eyes were on Freddie, making sure that he got in and got out of this situation safely. My role was incidental. These were dangerous steps he was taking. And more than anyone else, he would have known the risk. Or had he made his calculations? Did he know that he was too big for the IRA to do anything other than try to manage this day, and this embarrassment, away as quickly as possible? It was a roll of the dice. The numbers worked out for him.

When I think about it now, I wonder as I sat in that room on the Falls Road in 2003, where his handlers were, those from that intelligence world who had run him as 'Stakeknife'; those he had been in contact with those few days earlier when they finally persuaded him to go before he persuaded himself that he could come back, take his chance, look into the eyes of the IRA and hope his bluff would work, that he might get away with it. Surely he didn't take those steps without close cover – close enough to rescue him if this didn't work out? In the traffic and the parked cars on that busy road, where were the cavalry if he needed them? How would they know if he needed them? When we left that office, how did he leave? Where did he go? Who did he call? Did he watch the news that evening? This was the war in the peace. These were the questions that didn't get answered.

As I read into my files on this aspect of the dirty war, I am reminded of how the dead were used. I was taken back to some news reports and statements and a briefing or guidance in July 1990. Scappaticci may well have been stood down at this time. There had been another 'execution'. Patrick Flood was killed by the IRA, and a statement from that organisa-tion to BBC Radio Foyle in Derry included these words:

> His family should not be held responsible in any way for his activities. We would urge anyone working for the RUC or British Army to reflect on what has occurred and to immediately come forward. Irrespective of the length of time or depth of involvement, it is never too late. No one who does so has anything to fear from the IRA.

Flood's killing was being used as a warning. But it was also an attempt to encourage others to step forward, to step out of what they were doing. It was a statement of consequences that also suggested leniency in certain circumstances. They were trying to smoke out others by offering them a chance.

For years, it had been RUC policy not to comment by way of denial or confirmation on these IRA statements – a policy that dated back to June 1985, part of which reads:

It must be emphasised, however, that absolutely no inference or conclusion is to be drawn from the RUC's silence in individual cases. In the past, attention has often centred, wrongly, on whether or not a person was giving information to the police, rather than on the fact that a person was brutally murdered by self-appointed executioners. It is essential that public attention should be directed not to the RUC but to the terrorist organisations and the immorality and illegality of their actions. It is a fact that people who were not giving information to the security forces have been murdered.

That policy statement formed part of my reporting at the time. Then, on 27 July 1990, there was a development – a phone call with information to be attributed to a security source, stating that Flood was not an informer. I knew the caller, knew his position within policing. That line became part of our coverage and was picked up by others. A report in *The Irish News* described the challenge to the IRA claim as 'unique in recent years', while *The Sunday Times* reported that this 'unprecedented denial' cast doubt on IRA claims.

Many years later, I returned to the note I made of that conversation in July 1990. I thought about it and wrote about it in 2009 as part of a piece on the continuing efforts of then to build some 'truth' or information structure or process. I went through the lines of the note – a description in the conversation of 'exceptional circumstances'. Then, there was the line that Flood 'was not an informer – emphatically not'. 'They [the IRA] have got it wrong in the past, and they have got it wrong [in this case]. I would never, never, never try to play games with you.' From the content of my note, I have clearly asked why this was not being stated officially or on the record: 'We've got to preserve the policy,' the source responded. Today, I am still thinking about my scribbled lines in that note of 1990, their purpose, that 'unique' and 'unprecedented' move on the board. Why that call to me? Was it about it creating doubt in my head? Or about making the IRA question itself? This whole thing is a mess. Tangled knots, lines and lies, nothing straight, puppets and strings. It was the game that gave us Stakeknife, which I occasionally mistype as 'Stateknife'.

How do you determine truth? Find it in such a complex maze? The reality is we are not meant to find it. Not in these cases. We know about Brian Nelson, about others and about Stakeknife. Scappaticci remained in Belfast after those events in May 2003. He stayed until he could stay no longer; stayed until another jigsaw piece fell into place in March 2004. That piece had been in the background since 1993. Scappaticci had met with journalists from *The Cook Report* a short time after that investigative documentary team had made a film on Martin McGuinness, naming him as the man controlling the IRA. Unionists reacted to the film, calling for McGuinness to be arrested and for Sinn Féin to be banned. Gerry Adams said the programme was full of lies and innuendo.

It was afterwards that Scappaticci, calling himself Jack, met with members of the Cook team. That meeting was in a car park of a hotel, where Scappaticci talked about McGuinness and other republicans and their roles. He named Sean 'Spike' Murray, Danny Morrison, Gerry Adams and others. The conversation was secretly taped. And in March 2004 we heard it played on the Ulster Television programme *Insight*. Scappaticci, now, had nowhere to hide – damned by his own voice and his own words. His was a voice that republicans recognised. That night, after the programme, one commented: 'That man will never be seen again in the city.'

I watched the programme and prepared a speaking note for an interview I would do the next day on the BBC *Good Morning Ulster* programme. These were my scribbled thoughts written in that moment:

> I think the implications for Freddie Scappaticci are very serious. Because whatever republicans, and in particular the IRA, believe or don't believe about the 'Stakeknife' allegations, here they've heard Fred Scappaticci, in the company of journalists, before the original ceasefire of 1994, discuss senior republicans and their alleged roles within the IRA. And, in republican terms, that's treachery. And I think republicans will be asking themselves a number of questions. Why did Freddie Scappaticci approach this journalist in 1993 and was he put up to it? And, having heard him speak, there was no nervousness in his voice, no apprehension, as he talked so openly about IRA secrets, and republicans will ask themselves, in who else's company

has he done this? And, I think for those republicans who have suspected that Fred Scappaticci was working for the 'enemy', if you like, I think, for them, this tape will confirm their thinking. And, I imagine, it will now be impossible for Fred Scappaticci to live in west Belfast ... He hasn't been part of the IRA organisation for the best part of 14 years or so. So, he's been out of the picture for a very long time. But, having said that, the IRA is an organisation that prides itself on its internal security. And, here, you had someone thought to have been a significant and senior figure in the IRA's own internal security department, blow that internal security wide open in how he discussed a number of individuals with past and current links to the IRA. And, for the IRA, that will be hugely embarrassing. And, I think, something else will grow and develop out of all of this. Many people were killed by the IRA and labelled informants. People who had been interrogated by the internal security department of which Freddie Scappaticci was a part. And, I think, there will be those who will want to revisit those shootings and ask questions about them and about any role Freddie Scappaticci might have had in them.

The game of the previous year – his public appearance, those prepared lines, the denial, that mystery tour of May 2003, the questions that arose – that game was now up. We could forget about all of that now. On 16 March 2004 a republican told me that Scappaticci had fled; that police had warned him: 'This is the end of the line.' That secret tape recording, in the words of another republican, was 'confirmation for a lot of people that he was at it'. 'This will be the end of him on this road,' my source continued. 'He was a leading figure in this town, in the most difficult of years. He made stuff happen. He's not a £10 tout. If he was turned, he made his mind up to turn himself. They didn't turn him.' In 2004 the IRA was still out there as an organisation. It had not yet formally ended its armed campaign.

All of this is a part of the context in assessing the danger in that moment. For reasons they did not discuss at the time, and are not likely to discuss now, the IRA had played the game with Scappaticci in 2003. There were political negotiations that stretched throughout that year, working to put Stormont back together again. Perhaps Freddie was saved by the politics of that time. Now things were different. There was no way the republican leadership could ignore this. People had heard him, people who knew his voice. The IRA had heard him talking about things that he should not have been talking about. That is why he was gone – out of Belfast, to some other place. There was no more room on the stage here for his denials and his bluff.

We are still waiting to see how that team of outside investigators led by former Chief Constable Jon Boutcher concludes its work – what is called 'Operation Kenova'. Waiting to see how they link 'Stakeknife' and Scappaticci; what their report will tell us about those interrogations and executions that resulted from IRA courts martial; and what we will be told about those who ran the agents and what they knew. I annoyed Boutcher when I was interviewed for the BBC *Panorama* programme 'Stakeknife, the spy in the IRA' in 2017. John Ware was the reporter – someone experienced in walking his way through, and working his way through, the hidden tunnels of this place; able to find the things that are not easily found, and also able to explain the complexities of the buried wars. In conversation with him I suggested that this story is not really about Freddie, not any more. People have made their minds up about him. The story is to the left and to the right of the agent. What was going on. What people knew and what other people say they didn't know:

Ware: You think the inquiry will be closed down one way or another.

Rowan: I don't know. I do know this place. I think Scappaticci has the potential to pull the roof down on all sorts of people whether at the top of the republican leadership or whether within the intelligence community and beyond. And I'll be amazed if we get to that point.

Ware: Because?

Rowan: Because it's too damaging for too many people.

Not for a second was I suggesting that Boutcher and his team would not try to get to the truth of these things. It was obvious to me in conversations with him that he was absolutely determined to do so. But I knew that others would be equally determined to block his path, to hide the very worst of this place, and the very worst of that war; to put the information and the evidence in places of no electricity and no light and keep handy their thickest pens to draw the lines of redaction if or when things get to that point. Scappaticci is an embarrassment – or at least he should be – to the IRA, to the army and to the wider intelligence community – an embarrassment for those in governments who looked away from the 'intelligence war'. Those are the roofs that could collapse under the weight of the 'Stateknife' story. The 'golden egg' broke all the rules, scrambled people's heads. Alongside the 'human bombs' of the IRA and the loyalist 'butcher gangs', it represents the filth of war. Some years ago, I said it was too soon to be shocked by the revelations of the dirty war, because there was more and worse to come. It is still too soon.

With Nelson and Scappaticci we scratch the surface, seeing only a little of what happened here. Others know it all – the fine detail of these cases and how they fit into a wider frame. Sir John Wilsey is dead. But there are others from that military intelligence world who could tell the Stakeknife story; how it fitted into the bigger plan of things – that government mission that was the 'destruction of PIRA' – until there was a new approach, firstly, of secret contacts and then negotiations. Will they tell it? Not unless it is dragged out of them. Not unless the report of 'Operation Kenova' can find some way or route that escapes those pens of redaction. The truth of Stakeknife, or Scappaticci, is too damaging for too many people, not just in the intelligence community, but inside the IRA. He knows too much. Is it a truth too sick to be heard? Is that his escape, the real tunnel that takes him away from all those headlines of 2003 and the many since? Think of those who heard that clinking sound of a spoon on glass, the record button being pressed and those confessions before death. Think of the letters and the statements that emerged from those dark places, the interrogations with Stakeknife in the room, and the people who did not escape. It was the sickest of wars. But then we know that already.

# NINE

# A Rainy Day in Belfast

## A white envelope and an IRA statement

IN NEWS, THERE IS NOTHING like the build-up to a big story; the lack of sleep and the nervous energy that is part of such moments. With me, there were always telltale signs. I would pace up and down the BBC newsroom, constantly on the phone, numerous times with the same people. In the waiting there are busy moments, preparing the background reports, the type of in-depth analysis that sits alongside the biggest news. We were in the waiting room of the next headline, getting ready for 28 July 2005.

That Thursday, I was in the street where 'Tomás' had arranged to meet me. On this particular day, I was deliberately early for the appointment but, already, too late. He was hurrying, which was unusual for him – directing me to the back of a house. Eamonn Mallie was with me. It was one of those news days, except bigger: the day the IRA would end its war. I had taken two phone calls on my way to the Falls Road in west Belfast, both from BBC editors back in the office. It was unusual for them to call when they knew I was on such a journey, but this was different. The statement was already out, before its intended embargo. My Head of News, Andrew Colman, read me some lines and asked me what I thought: 'It sounds right to me,' I told him, those words sticking in my throat. I felt like I had been hit with a sledgehammer. On a day when I thought I would be leading on this story, I was now chasing it. News can be contrary. There are days when it likes to do its own thing, to step outside the terms and conditions set by others. This was one such moment.

That night, I slept on it. Or didn't sleep on it, and, the following morning, scribbled a few words that never saw the light of day. It was a story, I suppose, as a kind of penance – the news equivalent of three Hail Marys and an Our Father. I don't know if I was trying to make myself feel better or worse. It was a quick reflection on those events twenty-four hours earlier, that day on the summer calendar of 2005 that in all its contrariness refused to proceed as planned. It was a story I was telling against myself, me asking me for forgiveness.

As with all of these things, there had been a build-up. The drum roll of statements and developments that set the scene for something bigger. This was the way of the peace process. There were days when you'd get excited, when the news meant something, when you'd run with it and not get tired. The first real signal that things were moving was on the evening of 27 July, with the breaking news that the Shankill bomber, Sean Kelly, had been released from jail; a precondition to any IRA statement. With the help of my then BBC colleague Gareth Gordon and Kelly's solicitor, we had managed to get that story to air first. Gareth had spoken with the politician Jeffrey Donaldson, who had heard the news as it spread from the prison, while I had been contacted by Kevin Winters. I scribbled his information on the back of an envelope I found on a table in my mother's home. It would become the breaking news at nine o'clock that evening. We were one step closer now to the much-anticipated IRA statement.

Next morning came an interview on *Good Morning Ulster*, a bit of crystal ball-gazing on what the IRA might say when its statement came later. I said that, however it chose to say it, the IRA would have to signal an end to its 'armed struggle'. There would be moves towards completing the decommissioning process. It was possible that there would be Church witnesses and the republican reins would then be passed from the IRA to Sinn Féin. It was about political struggle now.

When the statement eventually emerged, all of that stood up. But how did that statement emerge? This was the part of the story I was telling against myself – my penance. I was standing in the newsroom when 'Tomás' called my mobile phone at around noon on 28 July. These were always brief conversations. They had to be. Just the basics. He wanted to meet within the hour, just before one o'clock. But he assured me that there would be enough time within the planned embargo on the statement to get things ready before broadcast. I was worried about only having a few minutes to prepare something for the news. But I left the BBC building for that meeting with P. O'Neill with something of a smug glow about me – something that wouldn't last.

The first BBC editor to call was Michael Cairns. The news was out – reports of the IRA statement. Then, within minutes, that call from Andrew Colman. I was in the street now, where I had arranged to meet 'Tomás'. He knew something had gone wrong with the embargo. There was no time to discuss it now, no point in discussing it now. We entered a house. I had been here before, months earlier, for another IRA statement.

In a sitting room, I remembered from the last time, 'Tomás' gave me a white envelope with the IRA statement inside. There was something else – a DVD. The IRA words had been recorded by Séanna Walsh, one of the longest-serving republican prisoners, who had been released early as part of the Good Friday Agreement arrangements. 'Tomás' wanted to show me the DVD but was struggling with the television remote. There was no point looking at me. By now, I was lost in the confusion and the chaos of this unscheduled breaking news. I moved to leave the house by the front door but was directed out the back – the same way we came in. On a rainy street in west Belfast, I immediately called the Radio Ulster *Talk Back* studio and soon I was speaking to the presenter, Wendy Austin. The copy of the IRA statement in the office did not have the P. O'Neill signature. I was able to assure her that he had put his name to the statement I had just been given. I got the DVD recording back to the office.

The BBC News 24 channel was first to broadcast it. At last, in that hectic hour or so, something had gone right.

Back on the Falls Road, later that afternoon, I bumped into Jim McVeigh, the last IRA jail leader in the Maze prison. I had met him there when journalists were given some access to the prisoners in 1998. And I had been there, a couple of years later, when he was freed. On this July afternoon in 2005, I asked him if he would be prepared to do a live interview on television that evening. He did and, in setting the IRA statement in its context, he said the 'war' was over but the struggle continued. This was the biggest IRA statement of the peace process, bigger than the ceasefire and bigger than decommissioning. Why? Because 'Tomás', Séanna Walsh, Gerry Adams and now Jim McVeigh all pointed to an endgame. For all of its complications and contortions, it was a remarkable day. I thought about that question: 'Where were you when …?' I was stuck in a house with a man who wanted to play a DVD! In the end, it figured itself out. The news was not about how the story emerged, but what that story meant. It was another step away from the war and another step further into the peace – a statement that at 4 p.m. that day, 28 July 2005, the armed campaign would end.

On a normal news day, with some time to talk, I would have asked 'Tomás' for his thinking on that statement. There would have been time to breathe and to take in those words of history – their context, their contribution to whatever would come next. But there was no time for that. Not in the unscheduled busyness of now. I had news to get on with. 'Tomás' had others to meet. He had been around the war a long time: in one of those balaclavas sitting beside a woman from the IRA leadership in an upstairs room in a house in west Belfast a few days before Christmas in 1991; part of that briefing which I used in a news assessment of the IRA as we turned into 1992; and I had first met him as a P. O'Neill on 13 March 2003, a meeting in a burger place outside Belfast. He brought rank to that position, to this new role, and it represented an end to the cold war of 2002, when a previous P. O'Neill had shut down contact with me in that row over my reporting of the IRA link to the Castlereagh break-in and to the development of weapons in Colombia.

There would be many meetings with 'Tomás' as the IRA considered and catalogued their contributions to long political negotiations throughout 2003 and 2004. These contacts with the latest P. O'Neill ranged from a few words or lines, to long, detailed written statements and briefings, reading across several pages, probably as much for internal as external consumption. This was in the post-Stormontgate period as efforts continued to restore an Executive. Both sets of negotiations failed. The first set of talks was with the Ulster Unionist leader, David Trimble. There were two efforts to get a deal in 2003, in April and then in October. In the latter, the IRA put arms beyond use, before Trimble withdrew from the sequence and stepped outside the choreographed agreement. I had met 'Tomás' at 11.15 on the morning of 21 October. I left a speech by Gerry Adams to do so and travelled across the city onto the Falls Road. The P. O'Neill statement ran to twelve lines. Its key sentences were that the IRA had authorised a further act of putting arms beyond use and that this would be 'verified under the agreed scheme'. Three hours later, in a telephone call, 'Tomás' told me this had now taken place.

The agreed scheme meant it had happened privately, out of vision, with only the IRA and the decommissioning body involved; that there would be no detail beyond that; certainly not the detail that Trimble was demanding and needed at that time to convince an ever-more sceptical unionist audience that the IRA was indeed destroying significant quantities of arms and reducing its war capability. Then there was talk in political circles that P. O'Neill was meant to have told me something more, beyond those twelve lines in that morning statement and in the briefest of phone conversations that afternoon. It was bollocks, of course. That is not the way it works. I did ask him that morning what was different between those two sequences, April and October. His reply? 'Ask David Trimble.' We knew, and reported, that this was believed to be the most significant act of decommissioning so far. But we had nothing on numbers of weapons or the weight of explosives. I had no expectation of hearing any of that. After being contacted by a number of his party colleagues, I met with Trimble in December 2003 to clear up any misunderstandings he may have had – to tell him face to face that the IRA had not given me any additional information. That meeting was facilitated by one of the party negotiators, Michael McGimpsey, someone with whom I had built a good working relationship.

In my extensive archive, I have written a note, a reflection on that period, with these thoughts on Trimble: that he was under internal pressure; that he misread IRA intentions in terms of what he anticipated would be provided re detail on decommissioning. Somewhere, someone had planted a seed that, along with its statement of 21 October, the IRA would provide me with additional information. This did not happen and nor had I expected it would. Trimble was being criticised internally, was under pressure and needed someone to blame. I became part of that. The more important and significant point in this period is that the process started to move beyond Trimble.

Weeks before that meeting with the Ulster Unionist leader, I had been cleared to make an interview request with the IRA, to ask some of the questions that were loud in the political debate and fallout of that time, including the demands for greater transparency on decommissioning and for a statement that the 'war is over'. That written request to the IRA was through a third party – a republican. The interview did not happen.

The following year a negotiation, at arm's length, with the DUP also failed. It is why the IRA moved unilaterally in 2005 to take itself and its weapons out of the political discussion and beyond unionist demands. After that rainy summer day of July, the next steps were on army demilitarisation and then decommissioning. These were big stories, big headlines, and there was no need for penance in terms of how they played out. On Monday, 1 August 2005, I reported on what I called the political and security bombshell, which was a timetabled announcement to disband the Northern Ireland-based battalions of the Royal Irish Regiment. It was part of a wider two-year plan to end the long-running military support role for policing in Northern Ireland – what was called 'Operation Banner'. The DUP heard the news on BBC radio at noon that day. Then, on 26 September, there was a call from 'Tomás' at 12.50 p.m. and a scribbled note in my jotter. These words were embargoed to 3 p.m.: 'The leadership of Óglaigh na hÉireann announced on July 28 that we had authorised our representative to engage with the IICD to complete the process to verifiably put arms beyond use. The IRA leadership can now confirm that the process of putting our arms beyond use has been completed. P. O'Neill'.

I posed a question that evening: Are these the last words from P. O'Neill, is this the last IRA statement in a thirty-five-year campaign? In this role, 'Tomás' would speak with me twice more, on both occasions in relation to the issue of the disappeared. There was a statement on Jean McConville, and then Joe Lynskey was added to the list of those who had been executed and secretly buried. Then 'Tomás' melted into the background of politics and negotiation, outside that war context. He was probably one of those whom the Independent Monitoring Commission (IMC) had in mind when it reported that: 'PIRA's commitment to following the political path has been further reinforced in the period under review with a number of people making the transition to positions in Sinn Féin and thereby engagement in democratic politics.'

It was a long road from those first statements of the 1980s to where we were now. None of these moments could have been predicted in the words and in the lines of those first contacts. It took more than a decade to get from the original ceasefire to those statements of 2005. The five P. O'Neills I knew spoke to a script, within a word frame that had been authorised by the IRA leadership. If they could be persuaded to talk in any information process, they would provide a valuable insight into the communications of war. There were thousands of statements, interviews, sourced comments, reaching back to long before I came into contact with that organisation in the late 1980s. There had been almost twenty years of conflict before then. Could they be persuaded? I don't know. I suppose it depends what we are trying to do in any process on the past. Would it be about reaching some better understanding of what happened and why – not just with the IRA, but across the board? Or would it be about something else?

I write more on this later but, here, I just want to make the point that, already, it might be too late. Something of an IRA structure remains, including, according to intelligence assessments, an Army Council. Within that remaining structure, there would be the capacity to produce a corporate memory of the war – its actions, the actions of others, that important context. Will it happen? There can be no certainty about that. Part of the post-2005 script is that the IRA has gone; that it has left the stage; that the war is over. What will that mean in terms of its contribution to any answering of the past? It will depend on how any process is shaped and on what it intends to do. Today's Army Council will decide how the IRA answers and doesn't answer. The past is not over. We are still fighting it – some would say to correct the narrative, others would say to prevent history being rewritten. There are those who still want to win, and others who are afraid of losing. In the 2022 context, some are afraid of losing Northern Ireland and the Union in the peace, not immediately, not now, but in the louder arguments for a border poll. For some, this is a different type of mental torture today: not knowing the future; not wanting to see it – holding on, but for how long?

# TEN

# Letters from London

*'I act on behalf of Her Majesty's Government'*

THIS IS WHAT HAPPENS WHEN you trespass into that world. Letters from London addressed to me started arriving in December 2007, in those brown envelopes with a window at the front. Some were marked recorded delivery; one, special delivery. They represented an escalation in a stand-off with MI5. The opening words in the first correspondence read: 'I act on behalf of Her Majesty's Government.' They are letters that you know you cannot ignore but still, I tried. My starting point was a 'fuck off' attitude, though not expressed in such succinct or blunt words. I was in a fight that would last for months.

In this chapter I am going to give one particular MI5 official the name 'Philip', to protect his identity. I made the mistake of talking with him, asking a question. It was the right question, asked of the right person, but before I had fully thought through the consequences of my words. What I spoke about clearly concerned him – he was worried about the fine detail that I had. It would be the beginning of this tug-of-war with the UK Security Service MI5. There were meetings and then the letters, out of which a request would become a demand. It was a warning, I suppose, of what happens when you dare to enter and explore and excavate those places of the hidden war, look over the walls, try to see inside.

I was having a bite of lunch with 'Philip' in the High Street in Holywood, about a mile or so from the new MI5 headquarters at Palace Barracks – that building that looks down towards the lough shore. These many years into the peace, it's a building still designed to see and hear everything; fitted with all of that gadgetry. One of 'Philip's' colleagues was also at the table. I decided to test some information, to judge his response, the reaction, and what I might learn from that. I knew there would be no confirmation or denial, but there might be something – silence, a look, an expression, a word or two. It was much more than that, much more than I had anticipated. The lunch, the conversation of 11 September 2007, was not the last word on the matter. Far from it. It was the beginning of the battle.

There would be follow-up telephone contact and another meeting with 'Philip' – the last one. This time he brought along someone else for company – 'Robert', another of his colleagues. Then, those letters from London began to arrive at my home address, from Treasury Solicitors, placed inside those stern and serious brown envelopes that stare at you, greet you with a dirty look and demand your immediate attention. There was red type on the front of the envelopes, in block capitals: LAW AT THE HEART OF GOVERNMENT. After some weeks of this, a senior police officer I knew intervened to try to negotiate some way out of this impasse. In conversation he told me that he believed I was 'squaring up for a fight'. It was not my intention, not when I started out on this, but it is what it had become. It was uncomfortable. At times, unnerving. It was an indication and a confirmation of how the secrets of the intelligence war still rank above all else.

The background to these developments is this. In Northern Ireland, in 2007, the lead role on 'national security' moved from the PSNI to MI5. This is when I first met 'Philip'. I was introduced to him and a colleague by someone from the PSNI. We met several more times, before that demand and deadlock meant that we would not meet again. As the story developed, I asked a former BBC colleague, the late Seamus Kelters, to get rid of some documents and notes for me – bury them, or whatever, just to make sure they would not be found. It was about protecting my notes, an unpublished document, and a range of sources, Special Branch and other police officers. The information related to the break-in at the Castlereagh police offices and then the republican political-intelligence gathering episode that came to be known as Stormontgate. I also had information on agents who sat at the very top of the loyalist organisations, their names and rank, one of them recently described to me by a retired intelligence officer as their 'go-to'.

I do not want to re-run all of the fine detail of these stories. All I want to say on these pages is that I came to learn of one of those hidden intelligence operations. This was back in 2002, during my time at the BBC. Just weeks earlier, as I was continuing my research into Castlereagh and other matters, I was warned from inside the police that my phone might 'be on', that an application had been made to listen in, and also to access my emails. I was later told that the application was blocked by then Secretary of State Dr John Reid. I have no way of knowing if it was or if it was not. It has been suggested to me that they did access my telephone records, which had shown contact with several senior officers. Why was I told from inside the PSNI that my phone might 'be on'? Because the person who told me was someone with whom I would have been in regular contact. He wanted me to be careful, to go quiet for a while, to protect him as well as myself.

As events developed, I would later learn that MI5 considered that one of my reports on Stormontgate, on 12 November 2002, 'presented prima-facie evidence that a breach of the Official Secrets Act may have taken place'. This was the night I first spoke the words Operation Torsion. I now had the codename for a major bugging and surveillance operation; a leak that caused ructions inside MI5 and the PSNI. There was considerable fallout, demands for internal investigations; fingers being pointed; a determination to find out how that information was made available to me, and by whom. One officer was made to carry the can for all of this: 'Forced out', to use his words. Special Branch believed another officer had done more damage. That officer would later find a file in a safe detailing his contacts with me. This was also the period when the IRA's P. O'Neill had ended contact, because of my news reports linking the IRA to that break-in at Castlereagh and to the development of weapons in Colombia. Next came Stormontgate. You can imagine what was going on inside my head. I was drowning in this, needing to think and thinking too much. Wondering who might be listening. Trying not to be seen with people. Taking advice from senior colleagues. Worrying about that officer who had walked the plank and being asked by a senior journalist at that time how I was feeling 'personally and professionally'.

Then we get to 2007. I am writing a book, including sections on Castlereagh and Stormontgate. And it is on this that I tested some information with 'Philip'. I knew he would know. I knew also that if my information was correct, he would not confirm it. But, as I mentioned earlier, I really just wanted to gauge his response. Both MI5 and PSNI Special Branch had known the IRA had the Stormontgate documents. They had been tracking them, watching a house in west Belfast that had been pinpointed by one of their sources, using those methods of 'alternative means of entry' to go inside on occasions. They had copied and replaced the papers. They had a bag made – a perfect replica of the one under a bed in which the documents had been placed. Inside this new bag there was a tracking device.

All of this had started with a 'small-time' source speaking to Special Branch, having some information to share with them and being able to identify the house where the documents were being kept. As it developed, it became something much bigger. He had taken them deep inside the IRA's intelligence operation. They would find evidence that republicans had been gathering information, including from inside the NIO. There was then a long wait, hoping that Bobby Storey would visit the house. That was part of their big plan.

Special Branch believed Storey had organised the break-in at their offices at Castlereagh and that his team was behind this other political intelligence-gathering episode. If he arrived at the house where the documents were being kept, then they would have him. The man who lived there knew the papers were in a bag under a bed. He had agreed to keep them there. But he knew nothing about the surveillance and bugging operation, or those occasions of 'alternative means of entry' when others stepped into his home, or how closely he was being watched and monitored throughout all of this.

The house owner was a sportsman. He would be away from his home on occasions, training, competing. And, when he was, intelligence officers were 'babysitting' him, close to him, always watching but not seen. It was this piece of fine-detail information that I tested with 'Philip'. I may have included details about the sport in which the man was involved and the high level at which he competed and how closely he was being watched. 'Philip's' response was that I should have the book read before publication, something he strongly urged me to do. 'Read by whom?' I asked. Either officially or by him, he responded. I knew what he meant. I could see and anticipate those thick black lines of redaction. I had no intention of allowing that to happen. Nor was I planning to identify the owner of the house. We called him Mr X. But I knew if this piece of information was right, then I could rely on the rest of what I had been told.

On 4 December 2007, when 'Philip' was accompanied by 'Robert', I was asked again for the manuscript. 'Philip' told me his concerns were the protection of life, protecting the identity of sources and possible breaches of Section 1 of the Official Secrets Act. My answer was the same. I would not be sharing the manuscript.

Weeks later, as Val and I were just about to leave the house to drive to Belfast for a walk around the market, the first letter dropped onto the hall floor. It included the following:

> I act on behalf of Her Majesty's Government. It has come to my client's attention that you are intending to publish the above book in March 2008. It is understood that whilst the book does not name agents, it may contain sufficient information so as to enable agents to be identified. My client is therefore concerned that the book might contain information that would put lives in danger and be damaging to national security. In these circumstances I am writing to request pre-publication access to the manuscript to enable my client to make an assessment of its contents.

I ignored the first and the second letters. But, although I didn't reply, I was speaking to people, working out what to do. I emailed a holding line on 9 January 2008. Then, eight days later, I sent another stalling line, before a more detailed response on 24 January 2008, in which I wrote:

> I have forwarded your latest letter to my publisher, who will respond separately. Your recent letters follow conversations I had with representatives of the Security Service. In those conversations, I was asked for the manuscript of my book, which I refused. I want to make my position clear. I do not intend to give pre-publication access to the manuscript to the Security Service, or any other Government department or official. Is it the Security Service MI5 who have asked you to request the manuscript? What are the specific concerns? When I have the answers to those questions, I will consult further with a lawyer, and may speak to officers of the National Union of Journalists if I feel that would be appropriate.

When I read back through my files now, I am reminded of all of this in actual time. It was a first in terms of this type of correspondence and the request that was being made.

Four days after my email reply, I spoke with the PSNI Assistant Chief Constable Peter Sheridan. He gave me a frank assessment: that the Security Service and Treasury Solicitors would take this as far as they could. His hope was that things might yet be 'recoverable' without 'fisticuffs'. The next letter from London was a confirmation of the Sheridan assessment:

> I note that you do not intend at present to provide pre-publication access to your manuscript to any Government department or official but that following receipt of this response you 'will consult further with a lawyer'. I would encourage you to obtain independent legal advice as soon as possible. I look forward to receiving your response as soon as possible after you have received independent legal advice. In light of the seriousness of the issues at stake and your reluctance to confirm the date of publication for your book or the details of your publisher, I would request that I receive your response by no later than Wednesday 6 February 2008.

This letter, dated 31 January 2008, did not answer my specific question about MI5. It stated: 'You will appreciate that a number of Government departments and other agencies have a legitimate interest in ensuring, and indeed a duty to ensure, that lives are not endangered and/or that damage does not occur to national security. As I have previously stated, I act on behalf of Her Majesty's Government.'

I received this latest correspondence both by email and by registered post. Things were clearly escalating. There were big calls to be made. One colleague advised: 'It's not going to be sorted through the back door.' Another spoke of the 'menacing tone' of that latest letter, while, at the same time, offering words of encouragement, perhaps even some comfort: 'You have been down this road before.' He told me to go with my instinct. I had been down the road of the fallout of 2002, my reporting then, the information I had, the tremor within the intelligence system when I spoke for the first time of Operation Torsion and the fine detail of bugging and surveillance that is always meant to be kept secret. I'd seen the consequences of that play out. There had been a convulsion of sorts within that world and then a blame game, in which, in my opinion, there were those who ran for cover and allowed a scapegoat scenario to emerge. But this was a different road with the letters. There were questions that stemmed from those. Might there be a raid? Could this end up in court? These were bends I hadn't previously negotiated. It was different, sapping – a struggle, at times, just to find the energy to think. I was consumed by this, keeping that manuscript close to me at all times. I was guarding it, I suppose. This, the battle behind the news.

Another colleague advised me to 'walk away'. He meant from this stuff about agents at the top of the loyalist organisations, this being one of the concerns MI5 had about my book: that, even if I did not use names, they might still be identified. 'There's nothing in it for you,' he said.

Assistant Chief Constable Peter Sheridan had not given up. I have a note of a meeting with him on 1 April 2008, 'Fools' Day'. How ironic when you think of many of the tricks of that dirty war, of how people had been fooled; those agents who lost their lives after interrogations conducted by another agent; and, here, in this moment in 2008, this latest effort by MI5 to shut down some more of the story. Such energy was being used to try to read a manuscript. What were they worried about? I knew and know Sheridan and the Chief Constable of that time, Sir Hugh Orde, better than I knew 'Philip' and his colleagues. And I knew that Sheridan was trying to sort this out without the headlines that would occur if any of my material was seized or any attempt was made to force redactions within the book. In a joking moment, a colleague suggested putting one of the letters on the front cover of the book, and another on the back. It was a light moment in a difficult time.

This is what Sheridan had to say in that Fools' Day meeting – that he had told MI5 that any approach by him would only be possible on the basis of the legal letters stopping. I told him that the final proofs of the book would be ready in May, that I was prepared to explore with the publisher whether I could show the relevant chunks to him, but that this would require an assurance from MI5 that they would not then pursue the matter legally. He said he would try to get that assurance. My offer was on the basis that nothing would be removed from the book – and I meant nothing. Only recently, I learned that MI5 had sought details from Sheridan about where we planned to meet. I don't know for what purpose or intention. By chance, at the last minute, I had changed the arrangements.

In the chronology of this, I had a further meeting with Sheridan on 13 May, when I gave him the relevant chapters. Then, on 23 May, we met again. He gave me a written response, seeking changes. On 11 June I told him again there would be no alterations to the text. 'None?' he asked. 'None,' I replied. In something that he said, I knew that he was unhappy. But, I guess he came to accept that my job and his job are different. Eight days later, he told me they would now have to do a properly audited threat assessment and advise those concerned. On this matter, I heard nothing more from MI5. There were no more letters from London.

In all of this, my dilemma was how far to push things. I could understand those concerns about the potential threat to life, not so the national security argument. It is too often an excuse for censorship. In allowing Sheridan to read the final proofs of two chapters, I was letting him and others make their assessment on whether they needed to relocate any individual.

The power-sharing government collapsed under the collective weight of Castlereagh, Colombia and the Stormontgate revelations. Could I defend my exploration and excavation of those stories? Yes, I could. And, yes, I can. My reporting of Operation Torsion prompted a battle for disclosure, for confirmation of those intelligence secrets: the 'alternative means of entry', copying and replacing documents, having a replica bag made with a tracking device inside, the story of the Special Branch source who opened the door to Stormontgate. There is so much to protect in that world of 'national insecurity'. On 8 December 2005, the Stormontgate case collapsed. The PSNI issued the following statement:

> The Police Service of Northern Ireland notes and understands the reasons given by the Public Prosecution Service in court today for the withdrawal of charges against three individuals. The entitlement of those three individuals to the presumption of innocence remains intact. The background to this case is that a paramilitary organisation, namely the Provisional IRA, was actively involved in the systematic gathering of information and targeting of individuals. Police investigated that activity and a police operation led to the recovery of thousands of sensitive documents which had been removed from government offices. A large number of people were subsequently warned about threats to them. That police investigation has concluded. There are no further lines of enquiry and no individuals are being sought by the police.

A Belfast republican, Denis Donaldson, had been arrested as part of the Stormontgate investigation. Just days after the case collapsed, he made a statement that he was a British agent, 'recruited in the 1980s after compromising myself during a vulnerable time in my life'. He described Stormontgate as 'a scam and a fiction'. It was a line that suited the republican narrative. Donaldson left Belfast and moved to a cottage in Donegal. I was told that two republicans visited him there a number of times, to question him about his involvement with the British, what he had told them. I am certain he did not tell Special Branch about what came to be called Stormontgate. And I am more certain now than ever, because of conversations I had in the preparation of this book. His arrest was because the documents ended up in his home at the end of a very long episode. The tracking device in the bag told Special Branch that the papers had been moved. So they arranged to meet him – their agent, codenamed Mr O'Neill, with the registration number 20/573. That meeting was to give him an opportunity to tell them what they already knew, but he said nothing and was arrested days later.

I have thick files with notes on Castlereagh, Colombia and Stormontgate – the 'buried' notes, the names, the watching, the waiting for Bobby Storey, that visit that never happened. There are thousands of words – the finest detail – including an unpublished document on the fallout within the intelligence and policing community; the finger-pointing and the covering of tracks. This was a consequence of that revelation of Operation Torsion and the intelligence earthquake at that time. Stormontgate was not a scam or a fiction. It was a republican lie in the peace.

The information that prompted Operation Torsion was from a 'small-time' source who provided a key into the IRA intelligence-gathering operation. It opened a big door, opened up something much bigger than was anticipated in the information he provided in his initial contact with Special Branch.

In 2006, Denis Donaldson was shot dead, a killing claimed by the dissident IRA. In 2015, a senior republican said something to me that suggested that Donaldson had not been killed by dissidents. It was another twist in the story; another line to think about. There were too many lines to think about, including how Donaldson was treated: the public confession, having to leave Belfast, the humiliation. Then, I think of Scappaticci: the public denial, a door left opened for him to stay in Belfast until a tape emerged of him speaking to journalists about the IRA and he had to run. Who did most damage to the IRA? Donaldson or Scappaticci? The answer is Stakeknife – the man who got away.

# ELEVEN

# The War of Lies and Truth

*For too long, these have been our tangled threads, with the past always choking the present*

THIS FAR INTO OUR PEACE process, I believe there is a need for us all, particularly those of us of the conflict generation, to take several steps back and to think about how we put the 'war' to rest; to understand and accept that peace does not come with all the truth and justice and reconciliation that is both expected and demanded, and that the longer we hold on to the past, the more we damage the present.

Peace can be cruel because of what it cannot deliver. It cannot bring back the dead. For many years, I have been a loud voice arguing for an amnesty across the conflict frame. It is not something I say lightly, or to harm, or to cause anger or controversy, but to try to introduce some honesty and reality into this debate and discussion. It is not easy to talk about amnesty, whether as a guest on the BBC Radio 4 *Moral Maze* programme in July 2021, or, months later, in Dublin Castle in the company of people who know the hurts and the loss of those conflict years much more than I do. I understand that every time I speak on this issue, I walk on the graves of this small place; that within people, this word amnesty stirs so much; that there will be those who think that I am trampling on the dead, betraying them, destroying the last hopes for justice and any chance of peace of mind. Yet, I think it is right to argue for a statute of limitations. I hear some people describe this as 'Rowan's agenda'. It is not an agenda. It is a different opinion.

Not for one minute am I telling people to forget or suggesting some drawing of a line. There is no line thick enough to draw through or under or over those 'Troubles' years. Instead, I am asking for a different approach.

An amnesty.

An information process without the implications of jail.

Practical help for all those who need it.

And for some proper place of remembrance and for storytelling, something to be imagined and shaped from outside of politics. Colin Davidson's 'Silent Testimony', likened by Eamonn Mallie to the Stations of the Cross, is one such example.

In numerous conversations, over many years, I have heard what is possible. I have watched as the most unlikely people have stepped into each other's company. I am convinced that there is a way of doing this. During the worst

of the 'Troubles', could I have envisaged chairing a meeting between the republican leader Martin McGuinness and
Chief Constable Sir George Hamilton? The answer is no.
But it happened in 2015; happened in a packed hall in west
Belfast, where both men were heard. There have been other
rooms with republicans, loyalists, police and representatives of victims' organisations present – hard conversations,
uncomfortable, but within which you hear the possibilities
for how information might be shared in some 'truth' process
if ever we get to that point. The answers are in those rooms,
if some way can be found to bring those informal, spontane-
ous conversations into a more structured format or process.
This, I think, is our challenge.

At times, our politics is still in the war. We have witnessed
this in recent years, including in 2022. At other times, it fools
itself that it might be our escape from that past and all it
entails. Politicians cannot shape this process, something
they have proved in numerous failed negotiations and
consultations. Nor can today and tomorrow be dictated or
designed by the families of victims or by survivors. It should
be work for others, from outside the hurt and the damage
of this place – for them to make sense of that war of lies
and truth, and to write the story with pens free of emotional
ink. In our waiting, the peace is constantly damaged by the
weight of the past, at times smothered by it. We need an
honest conversation about truth. Honesty, from all the sides,
about what will not be revealed. For as long as we fight the
past, the war will never really be over.

I think of some of the statements that have been made, that I have written down and logged over those many years of reporting this conflict as it tried to find its way to peace. Among them, in March 1999, was the first detailed briefing from the IRA on 'the disappeared', on people they had executed and buried, never to be found. At least, that had been the intention before peace came along. I was sitting in a car with 'Peter', the then P. O'Neill. 'Peter' was reading, me writing across five jotter pages. There were nine names: Seamus Wright, Kevin McKee, Eamon Molloy, Jean McConville, Columba McVeigh, Brendan Megraw, John McClory, Brian McKinney and Danny McIlhone – nine of the disappeared whose graves the IRA now believed it had identified after establishing a 'special unit' to ascertain their whereabouts. These twenty-three years later, as I write, Columba McVeigh has yet to be found (the searches that have taken place have not yet pinpointed his hidden grave). Then 'Peter' gave another name: 'As part of this investigation, we also endeavoured to locate the burial site of British SAS operative Robert Nairac. We were unable to do so.' Why were they unable to do so? What is the story of Robert Nairac and his disappearance, with still no prospect of identifying any burial place? Is it another of those truths that is too ugly to be told? Is it part of what will always be missing?

On the wider question of the disappeared, the IRA said: 'Our intention had been to rectify this injustice. We accept responsibility for it, and we are sorry it has taken so long to resolve.' Not sorry for the killings, but sorry for disappearing the bodies. Is that a 'truth' we want to hear? Or do we just want 'apology' – not an information process but a 'sorry' process? They are two very different things. That statement of 1999 could be repeated by the IRA in a 'truth' process in 2022, or some other year or time without alteration. The IRA manages and controls information. It is general, not specific; corporate, not individual. It says nothing about the so-called 'arrests' or the interrogations that followed: where people were taken, who they were with, what happened, who fired the shots, who put the shovels into the ground and buried the bodies. Did anyone say a prayer? Who came up with that unspeakable directive to disappear bodies, thought it acceptable, gave those instructions, allowed that to happen? Do they live with those ghosts and those graves? Many of the questions I have posed here will not be answered.

The 'truth' of this place is not just about 'collusion', now the dominant question in the exploration of the conflict period. Nor should everything else be brushed away in some passing reference, or some afterthought. It is a much wider canvas. It is the story of the 'human bombs', the human tragedies – those people who barely got a line in the news, forgotten as soon as they were remembered. The past is that virus of war and how quickly it spread through the 1970s, 1980s, 1990s and beyond. And the role of politics – its poison in all of this. If we want truth, then we need to look inside a fifty-year frame, perhaps something even wider.

When I think back now, I have so many questions that I know will never be answered, including about that loyalist

killing rage in the 1990s. I wonder at how political their
statements had become in singling out Hume and Adams,
and in creating that wide target that they called the pan-
nationalist front. There are questions about how they came to
have the guns of Ulster Resistance and the words to explain
their deeds. There are questions also about the specific
information and confidence they had, which allowed them
to travel deep into the republican community to target Sinn
Féin, not just in party offices, but in their homes. Adams was
among those they found. I recall interviewing him, down
the street, a short distance from the house, where one of
his brothers was carrying out repairs after a grenade attack.
Then there is Nelson's role – a former soldier, planted with
purpose inside the UDA, that still-legal organisation until
it could no longer be such, when the British government
was eventually shamed into proscribing it in 1992 as the
war was almost over. There was such a restructuring of that
organisation in this period, alongside that rearming, then
resupply. Something happened to make it happen. There
were many statements when false labels were attached to
victims, all part of this pretence of targeting the IRA and
other republicans, when what they were doing was killing
Catholics. Where do you find the truth in this web? How
do you begin to repair the damage? The type of truth that is
being asked for is not possible.

It is not just about the missing truth of documents that
were destroyed, but the many other papers that, deliberately
and conveniently, were never written: the thinking and the

orders on the 'human bombs'; those decisions to disappear the dead; the policy that gave us the Stakeknife courts inside the IRA; the horror of the butcher gangs and the UDA 'romper room' killings in which victims were beaten and tortured before 'execution'; the calculations about civilian dead – how many? – those balances in war; the politics and discrimination that helped it happen. All of this is the absent truth. And there are other missing pieces that are gone with the dead: McGuinness, Keenan, McKenna, Storey, Mayhew, Hermon, Wilsey, Thatcher, Haughey, Paisley, Nelson, Wright, Fulton, Murphy, Jackson, and those MI5 and Special Branch intelligence specialists dead in the helicopter crash of 1994 on the Mull of Kintyre. The list goes on.

If we are serious about doing something meaningful, something that might help, then it is time to sit down with the truth that is still with us, sit down with what might be achievable and with those who could make it possible – those we talk about and around, but rarely with. Politicians won't decide the truth and how it is told, others will – those who were at the coalfaces of our wars and in the back rooms; those who gave the orders. If there is to be a process, then we need to know what to expect in terms of their contributions. That won't be dictated or determined by others. It will be decided by the people I have heard in those quiet and uncomfortable conversations that I referenced earlier. They have the answers.

Years ago, I thought about the need for a conference that would bring all of the sides and all of the players to the one place at the same time – not just those with guns, but the Church representatives, politicians and media – and how they should be locked in together until some way is found to do this. That conference should be internationally chaired and last as long as it takes to work out statements of acknowledgement, the means of delivering information to families, and those boundaries and limitations that would frame all the 'truths'. There should be no court and no jail. That has been my view for a very long time. The generals, the chief constables and the directors and co-ordinators of intelligence should be in the room – as many of them as possible, stretching across that conflict period and into the peace – with Adams and the IRA, with the prime ministers, British and Irish, and with the loyalist 'brigadiers'. The party leaders (as part of the conversation, not deciding or shaping it) should be invited to it, but not issuing the invitations. The cardinals, archbishops, presidents and moderators must be there, along with the editors. It should be a conference that brings together those who practised war, those who talked about it, wrote about it and those who preached the condemnation. It should be a closed conference, at a level that can make decisions. Or we can stay on this legacy roundabout that has been spinning forever; in that conversation that goes in circles and goes nowhere.

My belief in the need for an amnesty is not some recent thinking but something that has evolved over a number of years. I wrote about it in the WAVE Trauma Centre magazine in 2008, ten years after the Good Friday Agreement; an agreement that gave no consideration to a process on the past and to this question of truth. This is what I wrote:

> Justice in the here and now of Northern Ireland or the North, is not jail for those who were part of Ulster's and Ireland's war. The peace process has moved beyond that. And whether it is called amnesty, or something less controversial, it is through a mechanism or process of that kind that truth will best be achieved. It will not be all of the truth, because some of it is far too ugly. Nor can it, or should it, be a process in which the 'good' condemn the 'bad'. The story of yesterday and yesteryear is much more complex.

How do we build on what has already been said? Those statements about what was unjustified and unjustifiable; the words of sincerest apologies and of abject and true remorse? Firstly, we need to answer why we are doing it. Is it to exorcise or to exonerate? To absolve or to blame? To win? To ensure that it never happens again? Surely this is what is important: saving the next generations from all that happened before and from these wars in our peace.

We are fooling ourselves about truth and justice, but, worse than that, we are kidding others. In some cases, we are using them, using them to fight the peace. We are running these long, protracted investigations for some, while throwing others a line or two, or a word or two, some scrap of information, if they are lucky. We have headlined the war, prioritised parts of it by assigning more resources and thus giving greater emphasis to things deemed more important. And, in that, we have forgotten those many others who need our attention and some acknowledgement of what happened to them – the little people, lost in a bigger play.

The five P. O'Neills I have written about in this book are still with us. So, also, is the man of the codewords and 'the crucible', who knew and knows so much about that killing surge in the early 1990s. Who knows also about the guns from Ulster Resistance, the contacts with that group and about the words that changed the statements of the UDA and linked UFF; about the arming and politicisation of that organisation in those times; about the advice that was given, and who gave it. Those other loyalists I met in that darkened room on the Shankill Road in November 1993 are also still with us – the men who were able to describe that huge arms shipment on its way to Northern Ireland at that time before it was intercepted. For all of them, the words of war came easily – the words before the peace. How much more difficult will it be to speak now? To answer the questions of that conflict period? A significant part of the war story is about the security and the intelligence operation, but there are many other significant parts that do not command anything like the same attention. It is wrong, shameful, that a continuing silence and cover-up is tolerated or allowed across the sides. If we are going down these roads, then it should be to see as much of the picture as we can, in all of its context. And we may find that we do not have the colours to paint it in all its ugliness.

It means a depoliticisation of the past in the here and now, and it needs that type of conference I described earlier, with all the sides and all the players in the room. It needs an amnesty to make the process of information possible and to remove the excuses for not talking – to take away the hiding places. There will be no legacy process until these things happen, at least not one of any meaning or of any worth. A resolution cannot come about as a result of the process outlined by the UK government in 2022, including a new Independent Commission for Reconciliation and Information Recovery. No one side from the conflict period should be dictating or determining how the past should be answered. The events of 1994 and 1998 were meant to represent the beginning of the end of the conflict. Any process that examines the past should not be some rewind button into investigations and evidence and information for the purpose of delivering people into jail. It should be about making information the closest thing to truth that is possible, and then turning that into reports for families. The naming and shaming of individuals should have no place in any of this. On all sides, this was a war of orders, issued from the top to the bottom. That also needs to be said by all the sides. Throwing a few more people into jail – the privates, the volunteers and the fighters – does not address the past. It is a way of avoiding it, an escape route for many.

What we have at the moment is something that is

haphazard and part-seeing. It is a shambles, a focus on particular events that often ignores what was happening around them. In my opinion, we need one report – not written by us – spanning the fifty-year context of war and peace.

Why would you release prisoners, allow the decommissioning of arms without evidence-gathering and create a process of protected information to recover the remains of the disappeared, and then continue to make paths to jail part of some legacy investigation? It is madness – a contradiction of what has already happened; a clash between the past and the peace. And, for some, it is this pathetic attempt to win, to win what cannot be won – the past and its war. For others it is about trying to salve their conscience, to make right what was wrong.

Going back is what my friend Colin Davidson referred to as the 'terrifying bit'. I found these pages hard to write – that journey back into meetings and conversations and situations and predicaments that stretch through thirty years and more. It is a journey that flicks a switch again, lights up places I would rather not see. I think about my mistakes, that 'biggest regret' that I described in that interview with Joe Austin in 2021, 'that we treated the conflict period as numbers and news'; that 'we forgot about people'; how that conflict dehumanised us; how the dead and injured became lines of copy, filling one news bulletin and then the next. The challenge now is to remember all of those who died, including those who died on their own, who didn't die in the big headlines. Is this what we are trying to do, when we look back into the past, when we lift the stones, when we point fingers? This place always needs help. It has needed help with politics, with policing, with decommissioning and it needs help with the past. It needs to be saved from itself. That means an amnesty, however hard it is to say and do. It means an international team to meet and speak with all sides and to write that fifty-year report of war and peace. It means information reports to families. It means providing the practical help that people need. It means finding a way to remember all of the dead. Then the conflict generation needs to let go and give others the chance to think about 2032 and 2042 and not 1972. For far too long, history and today have been our tangled threads – the past tying itself around the present and choking the hope in the peace.

# TWELVE

# David Ervine

### *How long is a political lifetime?*

YOU NEVER KNOW WHAT IS going to happen next, or how quickly it might happen. It was 20 December 2006, not long to Christmas, and I was standing in the home of the loyalist politician David Ervine. So, too, was a taxi driver, Davy Malcolm, who has driven me for years – to work, to news conferences, to meetings, to Stormont. This night, he'd picked me up at The Raven, a loyalist club at Castlereagh Street in east Belfast, and we were now dropping Ervine home. He lived at the top of the Braniel estate and insisted we should come in. I'm not good with dogs – terrified by some. Ervine's dog Troy looked to have a particularly big head. But perhaps it seemed larger seen through the lens of a few pints.

'Is it okay with Catholics?' I joked.

'It wouldn't eat a whole one,' he replied.

It was a year since I had left the BBC. Ervine had called me when I was in Belfast. I had arranged to see the then Chief Constable Hugh Orde at the Hilton Hotel. Ervine was not far away. He told me he was in the office, meaning The Raven. I called in to see him and stayed longer than expected. There was a good mood to the place that fitted the time of year. Ervine asked me would I do the Christmas draw, the raffle for hampers and such. My initial reaction was 'wise up', perhaps delivered in stronger words. The draw was real of course, but they were winding me up, knowing that I kick with the other foot. Behind me there was a portrait of the Queen. Two orange buckets, if I recall them correctly, had been placed on a table with the tickets inside. It was all conducted in an atmosphere of fun. Then, into the taxi and the journey home, via the Braniel.

David's wife, Jeanette, had called him several times. We were brought in to say hello. And on the way back out, I stumbled at their front door. I must have missed the step – I can't imagine why! Then, back in the taxi, I decided to call home, let them know I was on my way. But I didn't have my phone. So, I asked Davy to double back to Ervine's house and, outside, asked him to call my number. There it was, ringing in a bush. I collected it without Ervine hearing or seeing me, then called him to tell him that his home security was crap. The story of that night travelled. One taxi driver told another; Rene Mills, the wife of the second driver, then sketched the scene, framed it and gave it to me on my fiftieth birthday – me on my knees outside Ervine's home, him at the window inside, in his pyjamas, his pipe in hand, with words in a bubble: 'There's some eejit crawlin' about in the bushes.'

That night in December 2006 was the last time I saw David alive. Those few pints, that bit of craic were meant to be. We would have talked politics that night, as we did many times since we first met in the period leading to the ceasefires of 1994. And, on the phone, we would talk politics as December 2006 turned into the early days of January 2007, not knowing these were his last days. At this time, I was writing analysis and opinion pieces for the *Belfast Telegraph*. The focus then was on establishing the Executive of Paisley and McGuinness. It was still some months away. There were still some hurdles to jump and big decisions for Sinn Féin to make in terms of support for policing. There was also a continuing discussion about devolving policing and justice powers from London to Stormont. 'Not in my political lifetime,' was the response of some unionist politicians.

Those last phone conversations I had with David were about an article he had written and which he wanted placed. It was urging Paisley, in the event of Sinn Féin support for policing, to make the deal. Ervine sent the article to me on 5 January 2007, under the subject heading 'usual crap'. It had a four-word message: 'See what you think!' In our politics, Ervine was anything but usual. He was able to think for himself, think differently, say it differently; was not afraid of dialogue, not afraid of Adams or Sinn Féin. He understood that an accommodation here required all sides to step outside their comfort zones.

His article was published in the *Belfast Telegraph* on 9 January 2007 under the headline: 'Let's finish the job'. I had forwarded the piece to them. Politics was in limbo. The next moves would decide Stormont's future – whether it had one. It would require that once unthinkable agreement between the DUP and Sinn Féin. Ervine wrote:

> The next phase of the peace process is parliamentary democracy. It would be a travesty to get stuck at this point. It has taken a long time to ensure that politics takes primacy over paramilitarism. The establishment of the Assembly is absolutely vital to finish the job. Other factors – such as taking responsibility for health, education and the economy – are pressing. Being stuck where we are for any length of time is unthinkable. The endgame was always going to shake up the republican movement and its supporters. It is after all the final acceptance by republicans of Northern Ireland as a viable and integral part of the UK. It is also the final acceptance by republicans that no authority other than state authority is either practicable or tolerable. It is worth consideration for unionists, that if Adams pulls it off at the Ard Fheis [winning Sinn Féin support for policing at a scheduled special conference], a real line in history will have been drawn.

His article, including those words, were published the day after he died. On 8 January, in the Royal Victoria Hospital, I stood with Val at the edge of his bed, holding hands with others, as the Methodist Minister Gary Mason said a prayer

– not believing what I was seeing, not wanting to believe, not wanting to be there. We had become close friends. It was only a few weeks previously that we had those pints in The Raven, sitting beside an older man who wrote poetry on betting dockets, talking politics, thinking about what was next. There was no inkling of this.

In a walk in one of the hospital corridors shortly afterwards, I asked Mason, how long is a political lifetime? Not that David had been talking about that, but other unionist politicians were, as they set their faces against that transfer of policing powers from London to Stormont. The answer, of course, is that none of us knows. Such is the fragility and the unpredictability of life.

In what happened next, we could see what was different about Ervine – the respect that people had for him, stretching well beyond his own community and well beyond our small place. From inside the hospital, I did an interview with the BBC, probably while I was in shock. Then, outside the hospital, another interview with Jane Loughrey of Ulster Television. Afterwards, the first person to call me was the Belfast republican Jim Gibney, someone with whom I had first chatted in the period leading to the ceasefire of 1994. I remember a meeting upstairs in the Sinn Féin Falls Road offices about a week before that cessation was announced. It was dark. The windows had been filled in with breeze blocks – part of trying to fortify the building after a recent loyalist rocket attack, one of several on party offices. I noted our meeting in a few scribbled words inside my cheque book. There was some guidance as to the possible next steps. Anticipating the ceasefire announcement, Gibney spoke of 'The biggest story that has happened in a quarter of a century.' It was a week away. That close. A story and a headline as big as the one he predicted.

In the period after that ceasefire collapsed, I interviewed him a number of times for television, something he agreed to only occasionally, usually when he felt there was something that needed to be said and needed to be heard. One of those interviews was in November 1996, weeks after the IRA had shown itself again in Northern Ireland in the bomb attack at army headquarters in Lisburn, the Thiepval Barracks, where I had interviewed General Sir John Wilsey a few years earlier. Those explosions were heard from where I was standing in the car park of the Maze prison. Ervine was inside, part of a loyalist delegation meeting with UVF and Red Hand prisoners. There were around forty people in that conversation.

It is not hard to work out how the mood would have changed as this other news emerged. I interviewed Ervine immediately afterwards. I remember his angry words about the 'skulduggery' and the 'evil' of the IRA, but then calmer words when I spoke with him the next day. His advice to loyalists was to allow the IRA to destroy itself and its credibility in relation to peace in actions such as those inside Thiepval Barracks.

The bombs on that October day in 1996 put this place and its peace in greater jeopardy. It was another of those days when you just wait for what is going to happen next. The headline in *An Phoblacht* read: 'IRA bombs British HQ'. And the words beneath described the Lisburn headquarters as 'the nerve centre of British military control in Ireland'. With this place back in war, this is what Gibney had to say weeks later:

> What the British Government must realise is that the IRA were not defeated in August 1994. The British Government know that. Their generals know that. Everyone accepted that there was a stalemate, and what the British Government must realise is this; that they cannot get pre-conference table or at the conference table what they didn't get on the battlefield, and that is an IRA surrender.

Years later, when he called me in January 2007, it was to tell me that he and the former Sinn Féin Lord Mayor Tom Hartley wanted to go to see David's widow Jeanette, to pay their respects. Would I be able to sort that out? In 2002 Hartley and Ervine had participated in a film together, *Somme Journey*, exploring the issue of war and memory. As they returned from filming, Jeanette had driven Hartley home to west Belfast. Now he and Gibney would make a journey across the city into the Braniel estate. On 10 January 2007 my wife Val met them outside City Hall and drove them to the house.

I spoke to Joe Austin about this in that *Scéalta* interview in 2021: 'They arrive. I'm in the house. And, when they're

there, a number of loyalists arrive. And there's not a reaction
to their presence at all. In fact, there was the very opposite.
Thanks for being here. Thanks for coming … Those steps,
that they took … cleared the way for Adams to attend the
funeral.' I remember as we drove away from the house,
Gibney asked Hartley had he remembered to leave the
sympathy card and Hartley replied that he may have left his
electricity bill. He was joking, of course, but his words said
something about their nervousness in that moment – those
first steps into a different place, the difficult steps of peace,
not knowing how you will be welcomed or how you will be
received. It had gone well. Jeanette and others were pleased
to see them, appreciative of the significance and kindness of
what they had done. They understood that it was not easy.
'You had put it to me that they wanted to come, and I didn't
hesitate and they were welcomed.' This is Jeanette speaking
to me in conversation for this book. 'If they thought that well
of him [David], why would I refuse?'

Afterwards, Jim and Tom asked Val if it would be possible
to go back to west Belfast by a different route. In other words,
not back down through the Braniel estate, across the Knock
carriageway, down the Upper Newtownards Road onto
the Albertbridge or Newtownards roads. So, the way back
was what Val called the scenic route, and what they may
have considered to be a safer route. This was also a part of
the nervousness. Val drove towards Holywood, on to the
Sydenham Bypass, then into the west of the city. It was one
of those remarkable moments behind the scenes of our story,

something I asked Jim to reflect on as I was writing this section of the book:

> I knew from my own experience of my father dying suddenly, at forty-eight, how life is upended, never the same again. Death at any time is difficult. Sudden death is on another scale of grief altogether. I was eighteen and interned when my daddy died. Being in prison made it even more difficult. I knew that David's death would devastate his family. He was a big personality in the media and although I didn't know him, I got a sense that he was a big personality in his family as well. Tom Hartley was a colleague of David's on Belfast City Council. He felt it was appropriate that he visit the Ervine family home to pay his respects. He asked me to accompany him.

Gibney and Hartley are a bit of double act, always have been. They are the two men that Sinn Féin sent out to engage with anyone in the Protestant community who would speak with them in that period of the mid- to late 1990s, when ceasefires and political agreements were being explored. They are party men, Sinn Féin party men. They do things the republican way, no solo runs, no surprises. But this was different. It was something they decided themselves and without discussing with others, as Jim explains:

> The idea was spontaneous and a gesture of sympathy

to a grieving family. It wasn't politically motivated. Tom and I just wanted to let David's family know that he was being grieved beyond them. And in circles most unlikely. We wanted his family to know that republicans appreciated the contribution that David had made to peace. And we wanted to tell Jeanette that ourselves.

Then Gibney spoke of that journey that he and Tom made with Val:

We were slightly apprehensive. It was a very sad occasion and we were travelling through a part of Belfast we rarely frequented to meet people we had never met before. We were very warmly greeted by Jeanette and others in the living room. We spent some time with Jeanette speaking about David. And as we left, a group of men who were approaching the house thanked us. 'How are you doing lads? Good to see you,' one of them said. We returned the greeting in kind. We hoped our presence at the Ervine family home, at a time of great loss and sadness, helped them. It was an opportunity to privately and personally recognise the valuable contribution that David made to peace.

I had a front-row seat in that moment. And I watched those developments, understanding their great significance, through eyes that had seen the war. I watched from that experience of the 1980s and 1990s, when such steps would have been unthinkable, when my contacts with republicans and loyalists would have been about the last bomb or bullet, before the next bomb or bullet. So this was different. Very different. I was seeing the outworking of peace – what is possible, how the steps are not easy, but how they become easier. It was a reminder of how small this place is, how close the dividing lines are to each other, how little distance, but how much distance, there was and is between the different communities. It was also a reminder of how when something happens once, it can happen twice. Soon, it would be Adams' turn.

Later that day, I spoke with Gusty Spence and wrote a piece for the *Belfast Telegraph* that was published on 12 January, the morning of David's funeral. It appeared under the headline: 'Decades after they met in jail, Gusty Spence remembers his protégé':

They were men of the jail when they first met, one 20 years older than the other. That meeting between Gusty Spence and David Ervine dates back to the mid-1970s, a moment more than three decades into our past. Spence, the UVF leader, was there for murder. Ervine had been caught transporting a bomb. He was asked the question that Spence asked of every prisoner: 'Why are you here?' This wasn't about the bomb or the jail sentence. It was a question that looked for other answers. Why had he joined the UVF? Why had he become involved in Ulster's war? What next? Spence told me that, under his breath, Ervine whispered two words: 'Arrogant bastard.' It was the beginning of a long relationship that lasted until the death of the PUP leader on Monday. Spence became Ervine's political mentor. The two men thought and talked the same. 'There was a hidden David Ervine,' Gusty Spence told this newspaper. 'People just saw the public face. David anguished over things. The private face was somewhat different. It's the private face I remember.' In the politics of the jail, Spence said Ervine was 'in the front row', and that he 'didn't do hard time'. What Spence means is that he used his time, those five years in prison, 'always probing, always wanting to know why'. 'The talent was immediate,' Spence said, meaning he recognised immediately the political potential Ervine had. 'Politics to us was the art of the possible, and we could see no reason why we couldn't come to an accommodation.' Indeed, Spence was arguing that this was the only endpoint, that there was no alternative. 'We ruled out mass extermination and mass evacuation, and that left us, if you want, with mass accommodation,' he said. In today's situation, he talks about a process that is still on two tracks, the processes of politics and peace, and he believes the two will meet and that a deal will be achieved. 'The two must meet and will meet, and it's up to those two dominant parties (Sinn Féin and the DUP),' Spence said. 'It will be a strange wedding, but there have been other strange weddings in the past. One seems more than willing, while the other is rather shy, but I think they will end up at the altar of political reconciliation.' In those comments, in that language, you see and hear how Spence influenced Ervine. Their talking and their thinking were the same. 'We agreed a terrible long time ago that the day of the paramilitary was finished. [Spence] believes that loyalists and republicans have now 'faced their devils'. He said: 'David would never have made a good paramilitary, because number one, he was far too humane, and, number two, after he had seen the consequences of paramilitary activity, he agreed with those people in the UVF who were determined to bring about a political solution.' Spence is convinced that solution is now closer than ever. When you look for the things that have made that possible, you travel back to the ceasefires of 1994, first the IRA and then the Combined Loyalist Military Command, as it was then. It's been a long road since then, leading to today. And, decades after he met David Ervine in jail, what is Gusty Spence thinking? 'Whilst David will not be there, his message is loud and clear, and is the underlying theme which will bring both parties into government.' An old man of the war, Ervine's political mentor is starting to see a clearer peace.

That morning, at a funeral home on the Ravenhill Road, I spoke at the 'family' service. I remember one of his friends, Junior, from The Raven, telling me that he had slipped a twenty into David's pocket for his first bet upstairs. And me thinking quietly to myself that he was being cremated and that the twenty wouldn't get that far. The 'family' extended well beyond Jeanette and the boys, into the loyalist 'family', some of the wider political 'family' and the community 'family'. Then, as the funeral made its way across the city to east Belfast, Adams took those steps onto the Newtownards Road. Then, into the church with the leaders of the UVF and many others from the worlds of policing and politics. Former Taoiseach Albert Reynolds was there; Chief Constable Hugh Orde; the NI Secretary of State (now Lord) Peter Hain. You could touch the significance of this moment. It was beside us. You could hear it in the singing, in the words that were spoken. You could see it as you looked into every corner of the church. For all the sadness, there was hope. Val was with me and our oldest son, Ruairi, who had spent his days of work experience with David. There will have been some learning in that.

The point in the telling of this story is that those events, more than fifteen years ago, represented politics and peace working. Stormont was about to be restored in that remarkable moment captured in the pictures of Paisley and McGuinness. Republican and loyalist leaders were in the same place on that day of the funeral – remembering Ervine, celebrating the life of one of the true leaders to emerge in the period beyond the ceasefires, someone who understood the challenge and walked its steps. This was the most significant phase of the process since that period of the 1990s remembered for the ceasefires and the historic political or peace agreement at Easter 1998.

Just a few days before David died, there was an IRA statement. Published in *An Phoblacht*, it included these words: 'We believe that our political objectives can now be achieved by political means ... There are big challenges to be faced in the time ahead, republicans will not shy away from these challenges. We are very conscious that progress requires everyone to take risks.' There was a newspaper headline: 'Blair to the rescue', signalling yet another intervention by the then Prime Minister to push the DUP and Sinn Féin ever closer to that once unthinkable government. Then, David's words, written when there was no suggestion that he was close to death, urging unionists to think about and to understand the significance of any republican endorsement of policing. Then there were the risks that Gibney and Hartley took, then Adams, the UVF, and the Ervine family in accepting and welcoming the Sinn Féin president and his party colleague, Alex Maskey, to the funeral.

Within weeks, Sinn Féin had come to that historic decision on policing. Their path was cleared in an IRA convention at that time – a convention, eighteen months after that organisation had formally ended its armed campaign, and a meeting that underlined its continuing significance in the republican debate. Inside the intelligence community, the republican decision of late January 2007 is viewed as the 'landmark event', the 'pivotal moment', representing the end of the IRA war. Castlereagh and Stormontgate were now considered 'pre-watershed', meaning in the past.

I still struggle when I write or speak on the very personal aspects of that story in the period of 2006/2007, that last time I saw David alive, then seeing him lifeless in that hospital bed. The prayer. The walk in the corridor. That question: How long is a political lifetime? The interviews. Then, the phone call from Jim Gibney. His journey with Tom Hartley into places unknown. Val with them. Jeanette's welcome. Those few words of thanks from the loyalists arriving at the house in the Braniel as Jim and Tom were leaving. The funeral. Adams' presence. In June 2018 I told the story at an event in east Belfast. I brought that sketch with me: Ervine in his pyjamas at an upstairs window, pipe in hand, me on my knees searching for my phone in the bush outside. And, these many years later, people were listening as I spoke – a silence, a respect, an understanding of the significance of those events. And me, understanding the importance of this conversation I was chairing in 2018 between Sinn Féin MLA Linda Dillon and the loyalist Winston Irvine; looking into the audience and seeing loyalists Harry Stockman and Jim Wilson, and republicans Sean Murray and Séanna Walsh, the man of pictures and words on that DVD in 2005, when the IRA ordered an end to its armed campaign, and realising that even in times when things seem hopeless, people are still trying. The quiet work continues. This event was shaped by Professor John Brewer, Councillor John Kyle and the Sinn Féin Chair Declan Kearney – part of a series of conversations.

Lives were changed and ruined by circumstances here, by the sick politics of this place and the consequent conflict. Some thousands were killed. Thousands of others were injured. Many thousands were jailed. In our many conversations, I never asked Ervine where he was going with that bomb. It was something we never spoke of. I did not know him then. But I got to know him through those years that started to change this place. I have never had a detailed conversation with Jim Gibney about life in the 1970s and the 1980s. I went to his mother's funeral. He, with Hartley, was at my father's funeral. Winston Irvine was also there. The day before, he asked me would that cause me any problem and I told him no. On another occasion, I sat with former Methodist President Harold Good in a row of seats with Winston Irvine directly behind us at the funeral of William 'Plum' Smith, who chaired that loyalist ceasefire news conference in 1994. There has been too much blame, too many people with too many problems with others with whom they have never tried to speak, perhaps afraid of hearing something that might make them change their minds.

David Ervine and I could exchange angry words. He went through the roof during one of the loyalist feuds when I learned of some mediation that was happening privately, in which he was involved, and the BBC put a news camera outside the building. I have had difficult conversations with Jim

Gibney and with Winston Irvine, and with other republicans and loyalists. That is how it should be. None of this is cosy. They have jobs to do. Different from my work, but we speak, agree and argue, argue and agree. That is part of learning, part of building trust. I understand, of course, that peace is not a straight road. There are times when we lose our way and we are made to think and rethink.

By 3 May 2007 the UVF had formally declared its war over. From midnight it would 'assume a non-military, civilianised role'. We were arriving at that moment of the Paisley–McGuinness government, something that made us believe in the impossible. And we were close to something that was beginning to look like peace. On 9 May 2007 I wrote this observation of that moment in time:

> On their journey to yesterday two men have travelled a great distance, one through war and the army council, the other through no and never, and they've come to the same place. And in that place, on those seats in that Stormont hall, their shoulders touched. Martin McGuinness fought and ended the IRA's war. And Ian Paisley has come to the place of power-sharing. And, in their hands, those two men now hold our political future. This is the new era, the new beginning, and it can work.

But, as in 1994, we would see a flaw and a failing in the process – people hesitating, stalling and losing the momentum of that moment. The threads that were holding things together then began to fall loose. Paisley and McGuinness are no longer with us. Could Adams step onto the Newtownards Road today? The answer is no. The mood of now would not allow it. The peace process has retreated in that regard. Rewound. Gone backwards. Part of this is the post-Brexit fallout, the loyalist and unionist concern about the Union, an old certainty that has been shaken. Betrayed by a UK Prime Minister, by Boris Johnson. Northern Ireland is at another of those crossroads, at which this place is so often lost. The schisms within unionism; the leadership changes; one, then another and another. Add to this, the rise of Sinn Féin, north and south. The 'enemy' doing well, better than many would ever have contemplated. Not Adams and McGuinness this time, but Mary Lou McDonald and Michelle O'Neill. The 'New Ireland' conversation is louder. No one knows how near or how far we are to that destination.

Politics is back in that frame of fear. Change is coming. How much change? We don't know. But there is a slow realisation and understanding now that neither 1998, nor 2007, represented that 'final acceptance by republicans of Northern Ireland as a viable and integral part of the UK'. Nothing in this place is that final, that easy. And so we walk on difficult paths again, stepping on eggshells, walking on the dead. That damage of the war, its rubble, its pain are back in the conversation. The past, at times, is seemingly more important than the present.

In a casual conversation in 2022, one of the five P. O'Neills asked me had I had counselling. We were talking about how moments in that past still play inside all of our heads. The answer is no – not the formal kind that comes with an appointment. I thought about asking him the same question but paused – perhaps some other time. None of us has come through that conflict experience without damage. I have been lucky, being able to speak with Val, with trusted colleagues who know those times – the pressures, the dilemmas, the decisions, the doubts, that walk I describe along a path where morals and ethics are blurred and our minds become tortured. Being able to speak alongside others in those festival conversations has helped too, understanding that, with time, we can share more of our story and experiences, our fears. Writing this book has been part of that – letting people inside the mind's wardrobe, taking them behind those strict boundaries of news, opening a door. I hope, opening out another conversation. I suppose, coming to understand that not all this information needs to be inside that safe within us, locked behind some complicated combination. You can't allow it to rot there forever.

I want to finish with something I wrote about earlier – that you don't slow down peace. You get on with it. It needs energy and momentum, leadership, people who are courageous enough to take the necessary risks as they did in that period of the 1990s and, again, in 2007. Whatever is coming next, it will not be the hell of those conflict years. Talk is cheap. Many of those who are loudest now know nothing of the war, or should know better. You won't see them in the trenches of any next fight. They will run a mile, as afraid of conflict as they are of peace and of change. We know them. They know themselves. They are those who will leave the fighting and the jail to others. They are the cowards of war and peace. Might they at some point consider that the place to have the Northern Ireland conversation is in the New Ireland dialogue? And might they find that they have better friends here on this island than they have in Britain? Change can be difficult. But we know nothing is impossible. It happens when it happens.

# Last Word

*I wrote earlier that Val had the first word and the last word on whether this book would happen. She read chunks of it before I sent it to Conor and Patrick at Merrion Press. Of course, Val calls me Barney, as most people do. These are her thoughts:*

I WAS ON ONE SIDE of the bar. He, looking ruffled with his tie off and holding the bar up with outstretched arms, stood opposite. It was Christmas time, and his sister Kate had asked me to 'look after him'. He had been in a fight outside about God knows what. I knew he was a young journalist working in 'troubled times', which were to get much worse. At closing time, he waited and ironically walked me home, stopping en route at church grounds nearby to look up at a 30-foot Christmas tree. He learned I didn't have a tree and said he would get me one. I looked at him as he eyed up this monster and wondered what the next move would be.

Not long after, we were a couple, married and so our family began. So did his BBC career as a correspondent, and mine in mental health. He always joked he was correspondent of doom and gloom. There was nothing glamorous or easy about reporting the 'Troubles' and the atrocities that occurred on an almost daily basis in the 1980s and 1990s. Many years later, we would see how these two jobs would overlap and, in a way, how they complemented each other: him attending these awful scenes, bearing witness to the horrors, and me listening to the families recounting their stories of how loved ones died and the legacy that was passed down to next generations. To this day, the stories keep coming.

My second job, as chauffeur, was taking him to places for meetings and conversations with many different people from all walks and ways of life. The range of those he met was testament to his commitment of 'inclusion' of all sides. He had an ear for everyone, much to the disdain of some. However, he would not stop reporting as, in his view, news has to be shared. Stories that could not wait. It was worrisome; wondering, at times after he was dropped off, what could happen. He kept going with little fear, or so it seemed, and despite threats, huffs and impasse from various sources/ contacts that he built over years, he continued in his search for truth-telling. The war continued. He met 'generals' from many armies – senior figures at the top, others at the bottom and at the sides.

In later years, the cracks began to show, with sleepless nights and his worry about 'us' and family – the burden of carrying so many stories and the wonder of what to do with them all. It was in the 2000s, when he started to join up the many sides face to face to share their stories with each other. He said they were not 'cosy conversations'; indeed, having witnessed a few, they were definitely anything but cosy – but they were needed.

I worried about him, and often joked about him needing a safe place to talk other than with me. It was at this point, the Rev. Harold Good came into play to offer what I called his 'supervision' sessions – something, in my own profession, used to help lighten the load; a space to be heard and to reflect, and to make meaning of what is happening around you. Harold was 'hired' and is still a huge support to this day. Thank you Harold, and thank you Clodagh. Other supports came from colleagues, including the sage Seamus Kelters and Davy Morgan – both sadly gone. The list is long: Andrew Colman, Robin Walsh, Keith Baker, the real chauffeurs, Davy Malcolm and Davy Mills, and close friends Eamonn Mallie, Jim McDowell, Noel McCartney Davy Lynas and the real-deal Mervyn Jess, someone who has provided much-needed humour through the darkest days.

Recently Mervyn's wife, Lynn, and I listened as the two of them recounted some of the stories from the past; now at a stage in their lives and careers to reflect in a different way. It was fascinating to learn that they had never shared some of these before; one, in particular, of the killing of two young corporals in west Belfast. It was heart-wrenching to listen to Mervyn describe the difficulty of remembering the horrific sounds and images that never quite go away – carried in your mind. This was his story from the scene. Then Barney spoke of going to collect the IRA statement later that afternoon.

Reading this book, I am reminded of times when, in the middle of family holidays or events, he would have to leave because of the next piece of news and the analysis that was needed. The times spent at Drumcree each year; and the year that sticks in my head – the deaths of the young Quinn boys, Jason, Mark and Richard. We lit a candle for many weeks following their deaths and spoke about them at the dinner table with our own three children – all part of remembering. These were harrowing times. How did our children make sense of all of this? How did we as adults?

It is also important to remember the ceasefire times, the statement from the IRA which he delivered to the BBC, and how I cried when I heard it on the radio. I was almost nine months pregnant and remember thinking: are we to get some peace? A selfish thought perhaps. I remember the story told of Gladys in the newsroom and her nervousness as she typed that breaking news. I often think of David Ervine and Jeanette, the times we spent together; then, when David died, driving Tom Hartley and Jim Gibney to the Ervine family home; these different connections that join us up.

There are many more stories yet to be told. Families are still grieving, as they wait for answers that may never come. But Barney keeps looking, making those connections for others to share their stories, to help us inch forward and not return to what was. For us all, the learning continues. At times, it makes us mad. It troubles our minds. We travel on. We make meaning as best we can. We do that together. But we never forget, so we don't repeat the past. Thank you, Barney, for this book, one which I can truly say I've read.

*Last Word*

This one means more to me, because it's from the heart. It's about people and experiences and connecting, and that I understand. So, thanks for the last word.

*Val Rowan*

# Acknowledgements

I WASN'T SURE THAT I would write this book, with all that it would entail. Going back into the tunnel to walk through the darkness of that place. To find its ghosts. To remember again. The challenges and the risks in all of that. But perhaps we all need reminding of what was there before.

I sent Conor Graham at Merrion Press an outline of this book on 5 January 2022. I spoke with him and commissioning editor Patrick O'Donoghue by Zoom two weeks later and delivered the manuscript at the beginning of March – ahead of schedule. The words spilled out, as if they needed to escape. As if, at last, they had somewhere to run.

I banned the 'M' word. Memoir. Something way above my station. Far too grand and far too fancy for what I am trying to do here. This book is a very personal diary or reflection. Writing it has freed me of some of what I needed to get off my mind. Those drawers now empty.

Val and the kids, Ruairi, Elle and PJ, know the strains and stresses of my work better than anyone else. Those others I need to thank will know I am thanking them. There are far too many to list here – hundreds of sources. Those I contacted on numerous occasions to ensure that one piece of information was sound – many editors, my family in its widest frame, friends, the best of them Mervyn Jess. A thank you also to Dr Joanne Murphy at Queen's University for a line in an interview in 2021 that became the title of this book.

Val had the first say and the last word on this manuscript. Whether it would happen and how it would end. I also want to say thanks to Jude Hill, Mervyn Jess, Dr Joanne Murphy and Julian O'Neill for reading it and for their feedback and encouragement. I hope it gives some better understanding of what goes on behind the curtain of news. Reporting a conflict to the people on the different sides of this small community was never easy. Reporting peace became an even bigger challenge. Thanks to Heidi Houlihan, and to Wendy Logue, Maeve Convery and all at Merrion Press for turning these pages.

*Brian Rowan*